Very California

TRAVELS THROUGH THE GOLDEN STATE

California Poppy

WRITTEN & ILLUSTRATED BY

DIANA HOLLINGSWORTH GESSLER

ALGONQUIN BOOKS OF CHAPEL HILL
2001

Published by
Algonquin Books of Chapel Hill
Post Office Box 2225
Chapel Hill, North Carolina 27515-2225

a division of
Workman Publishing
708 Broadway
New York, New York 10003

Library of Congress Cataloging-in-Publication Data
Gessler, Diana Hollingsworth, 1946–
Very California: travels through the Golden State /
written and illustrated by Diana Hollingsworth Gessler.
p. cm.
Includes index.
ISBN 1-56512-285-2
1. California—Pictorial works. 2. California—Description
and travel—Anecdotes. 3. California—Social life and customs—
Anecdotes. 4. Gessler, Diana Hollingsworth,
1946—Journeys—California. I. Title.
F862 .G47 2001
979.4'053—dc21 00-066374

10 9 8 7 6 5 4 3 2 1
First Edition

To Paul —
The one & only
"Mr. Wonderful"

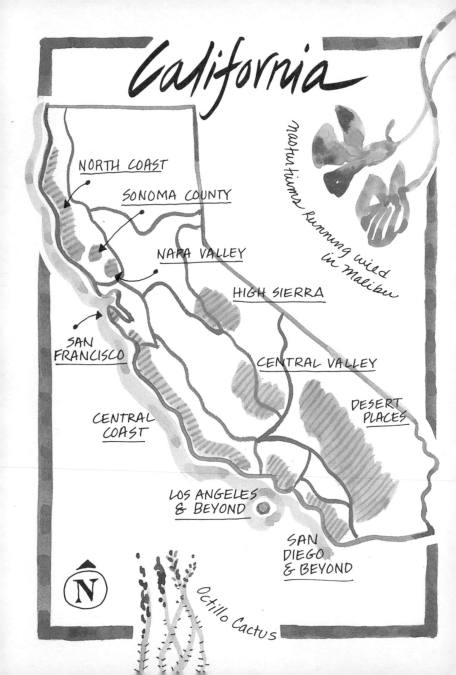

California

NORTH COAST

SONOMA COUNTY

NAPA VALLEY

HIGH SIERRA

Nasturtiums running wild in Malibu

SAN FRANCISCO

CENTRAL VALLEY

DESERT PLACES

CENTRAL COAST

LOS ANGELES & BEYOND

SAN DIEGO & BEYOND

N

Ocotillo Cactus

Contents

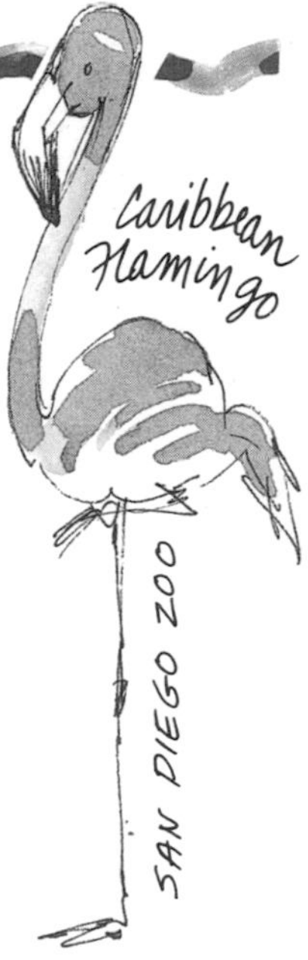

Caribbean Flamingo

SAN DIEGO ZOO

Very California

TRAVELS THROUGH THE GOLDEN STATE

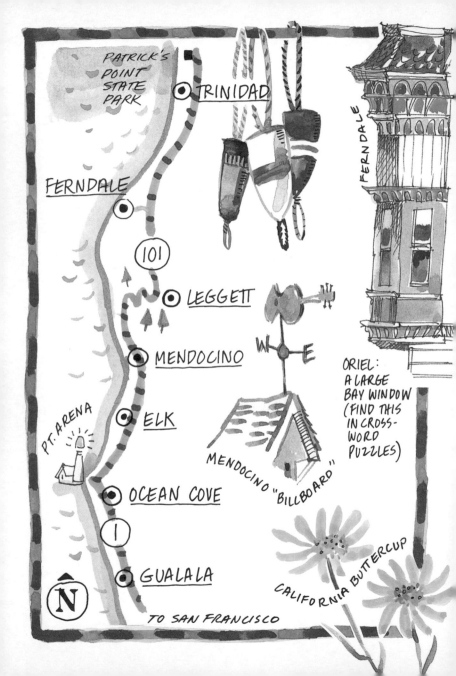

PATRICK'S POINT STATE PARK

⊙ TRINIDAD

FERNDALE
⊙

FERNDALE

101

⊙ LEGGETT

⊙ MENDOCINO

W — E

⊙ ELK

PT. ARENA

ORIEL: A LARGE BAY WINDOW (FIND THIS IN CROSSWORD PUZZLES)

MENDOCINO "BILLBOARD"

⊙ OCEAN COVE

1

⊙ GUALALA

CALIFORNIA BUTTERCUP

N̂

TO SAN FRANCISCO

A BICYCLE NEST

MENDOCINO

CHAPTER 1
North Coast

IF YOU'RE GOING TO "DO" CALIFORNIA, IT MAKES SENSE TO
TRAVEL FROM TOP TO BOTTOM. STARTING IN TRINIDAD, WE
RENTED A CABIN WITH A KITCHEN, SO PAUL PACKED SOME
"HERBS DE PROVENCE" JUST IN CASE. (SOMETIMES, HE EVEN
TRAVELS WITH HIS OWN KNIVES.)

WE HAD SEEN PICTURES OF THIS RUGGED COAST, WITH
ROCKY "SEA STACKS" JUTTING OUT OF THE OCEAN. WHAT
THE PHOTOS DON'T SHOW IS HOW BEAUTIFUL THESE SEA
STACKS ARE. NATURE HAS PUNCHED BIG HOLES IN
SOME AND THEN DECORATED THEM WITH COLORFUL
FLOWERS AND LICHEN.

Giant Vetch

FOUND THIS
FISHERMAN & A
HUNGRY FRIEND
ON THE TOWN PIER.

WHILE CLEANING
THIS HUGE SALMON,
HE TOLD US THE
RULES.

KING SALMON
FISHING RULES
- AT LEAST 20" LONG
- USE SPECIAL HOOK —
  NO BARB
- SEASON: AUGUST TO
  MID-SEPTEMBER

2

THE Emerald Forest
CABINS & CAMPGROUND

A BUNKHOUSE

ENTED A CABIN IN THE REDWOODS. PAUL BAKED A SALMON USING HIS "HERBS DE PROVENCE" AND WE ATE OUT ON THE PORCH UNDER THESE QUIET GIANT TREES THAT MADE US FEEL LIKE ANTS.

BUNDLED KID
TOODLING ALONG
THE BEACH

"TROLL ON A STROLL"

Patrick's Point
STATE PARK

HIKED ALONG THE
RIM TRAIL, WHICH
RUNS ALONG THIS
CLIFF... SHADY, SILENT
FOREST WITH
GLIMPSES OF THE
SEA BELOW.

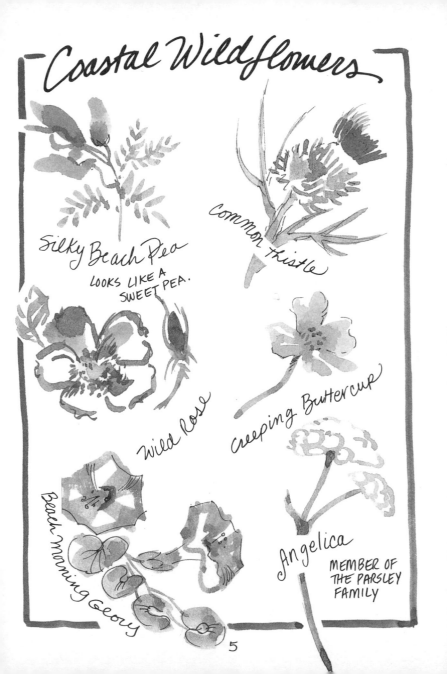

Coastal Wildflowers

Silky Beach Pea

LOOKS LIKE A
SWEET PEA.

Common Thistle

Wild Rose

Creeping Buttercup

Beach Morning Glory

Angelica

MEMBER OF
THE PARSLEY
FAMILY

5

ALSO KNOWN AS

The Victorian Village™

A STATE HISTORICAL LANDMARK

A Little History

1800's
"BUTTERFAT PALACES" WERE THE HOMES OF SUCCESSFUL DAIRY FARMERS.

1955 & 1964
FLOODS DESTROYED FARMERS.

1965
BECAME ALMOST A GHOST TOWN.

1970
ARTISTS MOVED IN & DOLLED IT UP.

LITTLE GIRL SELLING LEMONADE FROM HER PERFECT STAND IN THIS PERFECT TOWN

Lemonade 50¢
Rice Krispie Treats 50¢

I made the Rice Krispie treats myself.

LEMONADE

TOP OF PLAYHOUSE

"The House That Troy Built"

WHEN A WOMAN FROM OUT OF TOWN WON THIS NEWLY BUILT VICTORIAN PLAYHOUSE IN A RAFFLE, A LOCAL CITIZEN BOUGHT IT FROM HER SO IT COULD REMAIN HERE ON MAIN STREET.

Prideful Town!

Gingerbread Mansion Inn

A FAMOUS B & B

A LOT OF ARTISTS AND BED & BREAKFAST PLACES HERE

Victorian Inn
RESTORED TO ITS 1890 GLORY

7

LEGGETT

SEQUOIA SEMPERVIRENS

How To Grow Redwoods

1. PLACE PIECES OF REDWOOD (SEQUOIA) BURL IN A WHEELBARROW.

2. ADD WATER & SOAK.

3. WAIT... (2,400 YEARS).

315 FT.

21 FT. DIAMETER

The Chandelier Tree

WE THOUGHT WE JUST EKED THROUGH THIS REDWOOD IN A COMPACT... THEN A MINIVAN WENT THROUGH.

8

MENDOCINO

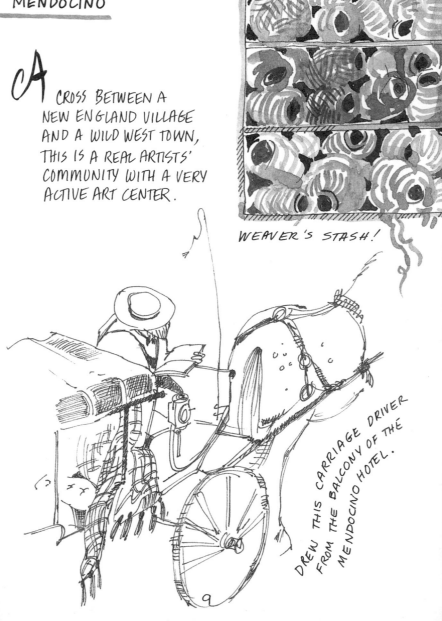

A CROSS BETWEEN A NEW ENGLAND VILLAGE AND A WILD WEST TOWN, THIS IS A REAL ARTISTS' COMMUNITY WITH A VERY ACTIVE ART CENTER.

WEAVER'S STASH!

DREW THIS CARRIAGE DRIVER FROM THE BALCONY OF THE MENDOCINO HOTEL.

PAINTING SEA STACKS WITH ALL THEIR COLOR COULD NEVER GET BORING.

THAT'S PROBABLY WHAT MONET THOUGHT ABOUT HIS HAYSTACKS.

LAND OF REDWOOD WATERTANKS.

THEY LOOK LIKE GIANT SCULPTURES IN THE SKY.

"ROCK GARDEN"

Things to Love About Elk

Roses

Giant Purple Cabbage

Garden Gates

an artist living in a parsonage

The View

HARD TO BELIEVE THIS WAS ONCE A LUMBER TOWN, OR EVEN A TOWN.

THERE ARE A HANDFUL OF BUILDINGS HERE NOW ALL ADORABLE & UP TO THEIR EAVES IN GARDENS.

11

OCEAN COVE

NOTHING HERE BUT THIS STORE, GAS STATION, CAMP-SITES, AND A WHOLE LOT OF NATURE

·1860·

OCEAN COVE GROCERY

ICE

THEIR BIKES

MET 2 GIRLS BIKING & CAMPING FROM CANADA TO SAN FRANCISCO ON U.S. 1 — A ROLLER COASTER ROAD.

AFTER 2 WEEKS, THEY ARE ONLY A DAY'S RIDE FROM SAN FRANCISCO AND A MUCH TALKED ABOUT MOTEL ROOM.

GUALALA

HAD LUNCH OVERLOOKING THE GUALALA RIVER MEETING THE SEA.

CORNMEAL CLAM CHOWDER

POLENTA CORNMEAL
FRESH GINGER
ROASTED GARLIC
CILANTRO
SESAME OIL
STEAMED CLAMS

(PAUL CAN TELL INGREDIENTS BY TASTE.)

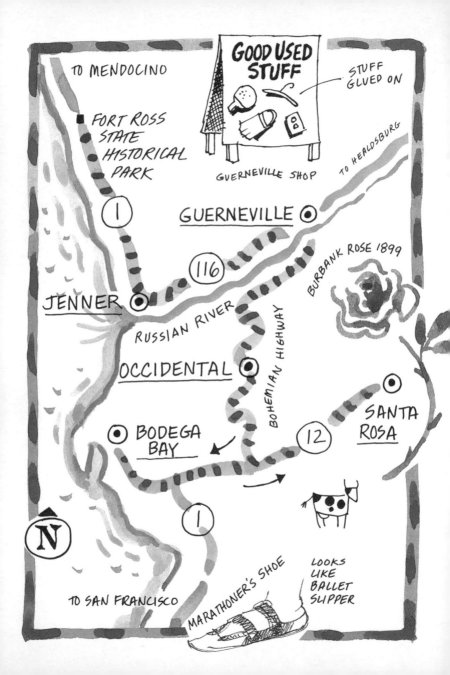

KITCHEN "CUPBOARD" IN THE FORT

CHAPTER 2
Sonoma County

IT MUST HAVE BEEN THE KASHAYA POMO INDIANS WHO FIRST STOOD ON A CLIFF AND SHOUTED "THE RUSSIANS ARE COMING!" BECAUSE SURPRISINGLY IN THE MIDDLE OF NOWHERE, SITS A DARK RUSSIAN FORT.

IN THE 1960'S HIPPIES CAME TO LIVE IN THE HILLS OF OCCIDENTAL. TODAY, MANY ARE ARTISTS AND ORGANIC FARMERS STROLLING THE STREETS AND DRIVING VINTAGE PICKUPS ALONG BOHEMIAN HIGHWAY.

AS A CHILD, I READ THE BIOGRAPHY OF LUTHER BURBANK, THE PLANT WIZARD WHO HAD A "MAGIC GARDEN". IT STILL EXISTS!

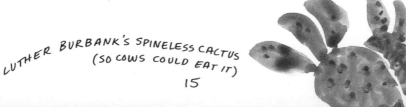

LUTHER BURBANK'S SPINELESS CACTUS (SO COWS COULD EAT IT)

15

Fort Ross STATE HISTORICAL PARK

← CHAPEL HIT BY EARTHQUAKE & LATER BY FIRE TOOK 4 YEARS TO REBUILD IN 1970.

THE RUSSIAN WORD FOR RUSSIA IS <u>ROSSIIA</u>.

IN 1812, A RUSSIAN TRADING COMPANY NEEDED A PLACE WHERE THEY COULD GROW FOOD FOR THEIR ALASKAN OUTPOSTS (LONG WINTERS) & SLAUGHTER OTTERS.

THEY BOUGHT THIS LAND FROM THE INDIANS AND BUILT A FORT TO PROTECT THEMSELVES FROM THE SPANISH, BUT IT WAS NEVER TESTED.

16

THE RUSSIANS HAD TO SELL
THE FORT IN 1841.

THE LAND & WEATHER
MADE FARMING DIFFICULT
& THE OTTERS WERE GONE.

1812: ONE OTTER PELT WORTH $100

California Sea Otter

AFTER A FEW OWNERS,
A LUMBERMAN BOUGHT
THE FORT & BUILT THIS
SLIDE CHUTE.

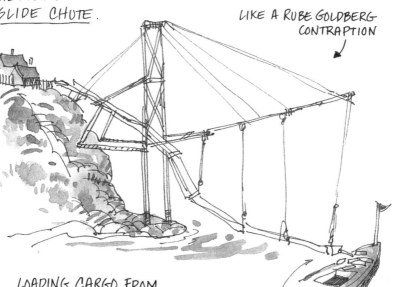

LIKE A RUBE GOLDBERG
CONTRAPTION

LOADING CARGO FROM
A CLIFF TOP TO A SCHOONER
IN A DOG HOLE (SMALL COVE)

LUMBER

17

a new Perspective on Space

THOUGHT IT WAS A SHORT WALK TO THE BARKING SEA LIONS.

WALKED FOREVER... SURE ENOUGH, FORT WAS FARAWAY.

BUT... THE SEA WAS EQUALLY FAR AWAY...

WE HAD BEEN SWALLOWED UP BY THE EXPANSE.

California Sea Lions have no manes.

SOME OF THE NATIVE ALASKANS BROUGHT HERE BY THE RUSSIANS TO BUILD THE FORT & HUNT SEA OTTERS WERE ALEUTS.

WHILE HUNTING SEA OTTERS, THEY USED THINGS MADE FROM

SEA LIONS.

Skins - COVERED THEIR BAIDARKAS (KAYAKS)

Intestines - MADE INTO WATERPROOF CLOTHING

Whiskers - DECORATED THEIR WOODEN HATS

SHIELDS EYES WHILE HUNTING.

19

JENNER

LAST NIGHT'S FULL MOON

FOG BANK

RUSSIAN RIVER →

LONE KAYAKER

*H*AVING COFFEE ON A PICNIC BENCH & WATCHING THE MORNING UNFOLD

THE PACIFIC

RUSSIAN RIVER

HARBOR SEAL

SOME SEALS WERE BELLY UP ON THE SAND (LIKE WHITE SLUGS) WHILE OTHERS PLAYED IN THE RIVER.

20

GUERNEVILLE

WE WERE WALKING
THE TOWN EARLY IN THE
MORNING WHEN BIKES
CAME SWOOSHING BY —
WE FOLLOWED THEIR
TRAIL TO THE ICE-COLD
RUSSIAN RIVER (72°).

The Vineman
TRIATHLON

SWIM: 2.4 MILES
BIKE: 112 MILES
RUN: 26.2 MILES

SKIN-
TIGHT
WET
SUIT

AFTER THE
SWIM

PEELING —
NO HELP ALLOWED

WHAT'S
UNDERNEATH

JUST 5 HOURS
TO GO.

THIS POOR
GUY HAD A FLAT BEFORE HE
STARTED THE
BIKE
LEG.

OLD
TIRE

I Have 3 kids
in this. They
want 3 subs
each tonight.

MOTHER

21

OCCIDENTAL

ODD NAME FOR AN ODD TOWN

MEANS "WESTERN" AS OPPOSED TO ORIENTAL

KNOWN FOR ITS HIPPIES AND ITS ITALIAN FOOD ~ THE SMELL OF RED SAUCE IS EVERYWHERE.

LOCAL CHARACTER

"RANGER RICK" ROAMS THE TOWN. SAID I WASN'T FAST ENOUGH TO DRAW HIM...

SIGN OVER A BAR DOOR

OCCIDENTAL YACHT CLUB
OYC

AT LAST! A CLUB FOR MARTINI DRINKERS WHO ARE SURROUNDED BY MOUNTAINS & CAN'T GET TO THEIR YACHTS.

Looks like a Grapes of Wrath move.

HIPPIE

PAUL

WICKER PORCH CHAIR
OAK BOOKCASE
SATELLITE DISH
CLUNKY PICKUP ON ITS LAST MOVE!

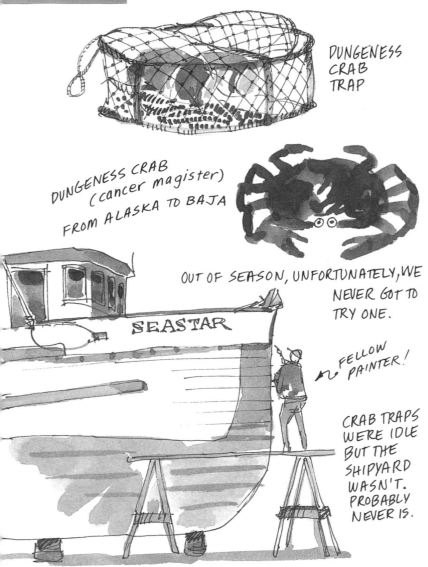

DUNGENESS
CRAB
TRAP

DUNGENESS CRAB
(cancer magister)
FROM ALASKA TO BAJA

OUT OF SEASON, UNFORTUNATELY, WE
NEVER GOT TO
TRY ONE.

SEASTAR

FELLOW
PAINTER!

CRAB TRAPS
WERE IDLE
BUT THE
SHIPYARD
WASN'T.
PROBABLY
NEVER IS.

The LUTHER BURBANK

HOME & GARDENS

A WORLD FAMOUS
HORTICULTURALIST—
HIS GARDEN
WAS HIS
LAB.

24

LUTHER BURBANK 1849-1926

shasta Daisy

ONE OF HIS BEST-KNOWN
CREATIONS:

HE CROSSED THE OXEYE
DAISY WITH 2 EUROPEAN
DAISIES. AND FOR WHITENESS,
ADDED THE JAPANESE NIPON
AS A POLLEN PARENT.

NAMED AFTER THE WHITE-
CAPPED MT. SHASTA IN
NORTHERN CALIFORNIA.

"FRAGRANCE"

HE MADE
A CALLA LILY WITH
A SWEET SMELL.

PARADOX WALNUT

BURBANK TOOK A
SLOW GROWING WALNUT
TREE & MADE IT GROW
FAST, THUS THE
NAME "PARADOX."

MUSEUM THOUGHT
IT WAS DEAD &
CUT OFF A BRANCH.
IT WAS ALIVE.
OOPS!

The secret to plant breeding is love.
LUTHER BURBANK

"MOOD INDIGO"

HE ENHANCED THE
AGAPANTHUS
Lily-of-the-Nile
SEEMS TO BE
CALIFORNIA'S FAVORITE —
IT'S PROFUSE.

LUTHER BURBANK PRIDED HIMSELF ON COOKING
"TURKEY A LA BURBANK",
WITH A SPECIAL STUFFING THAT INCLUDED BREAD:

"... BUTTER EACH SLICE AS A HUNGRY
BOY WOULD LIKE IT."

BUT
"... ADD NO OYSTERS, EGGS, CHESTNUTS,
OR OTHER ABOMINATIONS."

BACON
STRIPS

Juillard Park

ACROSS FROM
BURBANK'S
HOME...
BIG TREES
AND
STREAMS

OUR PICNIC CLOTH FROM PROVENCE

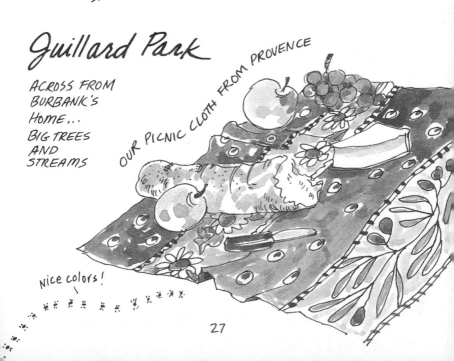

Nice colors!

SMACK IN THE MIDDLE OF COSMOS & SUNFLOWERS

CHAPTER 3

Napa Valley

NAPA HAD BEEN ON OUR "TO DO" LIST FOR A LONG
TIME. BUT WE THOUGHT WHEN IT CAME TO
VINEYARDS, WE'D "BEEN THERE, DONE THAT." WRONG.

WE BEGAN READING ABOUT VINEYARDS LIKE NEIBAUM-
COPPOLA AND LEARNING ABOUT "RUTHERFORD DUST"
(THE TASTE SENSATION IN A GLASS OF RUBICON WINE).
EARLY VINTNERS CALLED THIS A "HEAVENLY PLACE" AND A
"COZY CORNER" ("INGLENOOK" IN SCOTTISH).

ANOTHER SURPRISE WAS THE CULINARY INSTITUTE
OF AMERICA AT GREYSTONE. PAUL HAD HEARD OF IT,
BUT WE THOUGHT IT WAS JUST A SCHOOL. WRONG AGAIN.
FOR US, IT WAS THE SECRET OF NAPA.

CALISTOGA

SAM BRANNAN
(A MILLIONAIRE AT 33)
BUILT A HOT SPRINGS
COTTAGE RESORT
HERE IN 1860.
IT'S GONE NOW.

IT IS SAID HE
COMBINED THE
NAME SARATOGA
& CALIFORNIA.

STUFFED
MUSEUM
PIECE

HOW HENS
MUST HAVE
DONE IT
IN THE
1800's?

She's got all her eggs in one basket.

THE
SHARPSTEEN
MUSEUM
& SAM BRANNAN COTTAGE

INSIDE ARE BEAUTIFULLY DETAILED
AND ARTISTIC DIORAMAS DEPICTING
CALISTOGA IN THE 1800's.

← THIS DRAWING IS
FROM BRANNAN'S
RESORT DIORAMA.

THERE IS AN
ORIGINAL
COTTAGE NEXT
TO THE MUSEUM.

GREYSTONE

THE CULINARY INSTITUTE OF AMERICA (C.I.A.) HAS ITS WEST COAST CONTINUING EDUCATION CENTER ON THIS ESTATE.

A WINE CO-OP CALLED "GREYSTONE CELLARS" IN 1888... & THE NAME STUCK.

THE STAR IS THE SYMBOL OF GREYSTONE.

WHEN THE BUILDING WAS RETROFITTED (TO EARTH-QUAKE PROOF), IRON STARS WERE USED AS WASHERS AT THE ENDS OF TIE RODS.

GREYSTONE IS STAR-STUDDED INSIDE & OUT.

Cellar Keys

31

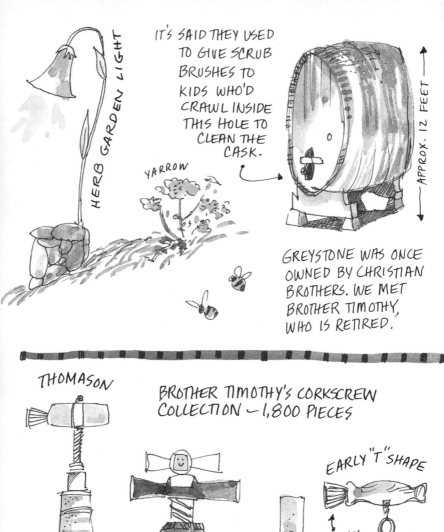

HERB GARDEN LIGHT

IT'S SAID THEY USED TO GIVE SCRUB BRUSHES TO KIDS WHO'D CRAWL INSIDE THIS HOLE TO CLEAN THE CASK.

YARROW

APPROX. 12 FEET

GREYSTONE WAS ONCE OWNED BY CHRISTIAN BROTHERS. WE MET BROTHER TIMOTHY, WHO IS RETIRED.

THOMASON

BROTHER TIMOTHY'S CORKSCREW COLLECTION — 1,800 PIECES

EARLY "T" SHAPE

BRUSH

DESIGN 1802

SPINACH SPAETZLE

KitchenViewing Tour

WATCHING EXECUTIVE CHEFS FROM MARRIOTT TAKING "REFRESHER" COURSES

MODERN GONG/SCULPTURE IN THE KITCHEN

← MALLET

WHEN THE GONG SOUNDS, EVERYONE EATS.

STUDENTS ARE GIVEN VARIOUS RECIPES. TODAY'S THEME:

"Fusion"

AT NOON, THEIR WORK IS DISPLAYED ON THIS TABLE & CRITIQUED.

ALL DISHES ARE UNIQUE, DOWN TO THE CHINA PATTERNS.

The Silverado Museum

A PERSONAL COLLECTION OF ROBERT LOUIS STEVENSON STUFF.

INCLUDES HIS LEAD SOLDIERS FROM CHILDHOOD.

...THE INSPIRATION FOR "LAND OF COUNTERPANE"

*F*ANNY WAS A DIVORCED ARTIST WITH DETERMINATION. NURSED LOUIS'S FRAIL HEALTH UNTIL HE DIED. THEN SHE PUBLISHED HIS...

A CHILD'S GARDEN OF VERSES

...FROM WORK SHE HAD RETRIEVED FROM HIS WASTEBASKET OVER THE YEARS.

LAST PHOTO TAKEN IN 1894

Fanny Osbourne Stevenson

Adagio Bed & Breakfast

NEW OWNERS — WE WERE THEIR FIRST GUESTS.

Lemon Muffins

MIX & SET ASIDE:
2 cups white flour
3/4 cup sugar
3/4 tsp. baking soda
1 tsp. baking powder
1/4 tsp. salt

MIX TOGETHER:
8 oz. lemon yogurt
1/3 cup canola oil
1 egg
zest from 2 lemons (chopped fine)
2 capfuls of lemon extract

GLAZE INGREDIENTS: 1/2 cup lemon juice, 1/2 cup sugar.
30-40 seconds in microwave until sugar dissolved.

Combine wet and dry ingredients. For uniform muffin size, use an ice cream scoop and scoop into greased muffin tins. Brush tops with lemon glaze. Bake at 375°F for approximately 20 minutes. Turn at 10 minutes for even browning. (yield 12 muffins)

A FIGLEAF YELLOWED AND FELL…

NOW I KNOW WHY THEY WERE USED IN EDEN — THEY'RE <u>HUGE</u>.

DINING UNDER A TWINKLING FIG TREE IN THE GARDEN AT SHOWLEY'S RESTAURANT

ARTICHOKE STUFFED WITH BREAD CRUMBS AND DIPPING SAUCES IN A NAPKIN "PLATE"

(SMALL CUPS TUCKED INTO FOLDS OF A BIG NAPKIN)

The Napa Palette

COBALT BLUE SKY

LAVENDER MOUNTAINS

EMERALD FOREST

LIME GREEN VINEYARDS

ORANGE WEEDS/GRASSES

PURPLE "LAVENDER" BUSHES

Sunflower

RUTHERFORD

A Roadside Stand

← ME

OPEN

PAUL PICKING OUT
FRUITS & VEGETABLES
FOR OUR PICNIC.

WHEN I STOOD IN THE
FIELDS OF COSMOS &
SUNFLOWERS, I WAS
IN COLOR HEAVEN.

39

niebaum~ Coppola WINERY

OLD STONE WINERY

GIFT SHOP: BOUGHT A TABLECLOTH & A NAPA "MUST"~ A NEW STRAW HAT.

Peppery on the finish, berries on the nose.

THE MAN WHO POURED THE "TASTINGS" TALKING ABOUT BLACK LABEL CLARET

I Didn't know anyone talked like that.

St. Supéry

VINEYARDS & WINERY

WE TASTED THE ST. SUPÉRY 1998 SAUVIGNON BLANC AT GREYSTONE & JUST HAD TO COME HERE FOR MORE, EVEN THOUGH IT WAS 10:00 A.M.

COMPUTERIZED VINEYARD WEATHER STATION

WITH ITS WHITE SHUTTERS, IT LOOKS LIKE A VICTORIAN DOVE COOP.

READINGS GO TO THE MASTER COMPUTER ON THE HALF HOUR.

California Quail

SINGS A DIFFERENT TUNE FROM THE BOB WHITE QUAIL.

41

BODIE "STREET SCULPTURE"

CHAPTER 4

High Sierra

WE FELT LIKE WE HIT THE "MOTHER LODE" IN FINDING THIS ROUTE THROUGH GOLD COUNTRY AND THE HIGH SIERRA.

COLUMBIA'S MAIN STREET IS A WORKING 1850'S GOLD-RUSH TOWN, WITH PRESENT-DAY HOMES JUST A BLOCK AWAY. WE HAD HEARD OF THE MAJESTY OF YOSEMITE, BUT BECAME ENCHANTED BY THE LIGHT GREEN, FLOWER-FILLED MEADOWS.

BUT BODIE IS THE REAL TREASURE ⁓ A GHOST TOWN KEPT IN A STATE OF "ARRESTED DECAY." IT HAD SUCH A REPUTATION FOR ITS WICKEDNESS AND WEATHER (EXTREME) THAT IN THE 1800'S, A LITTLE GIRL WROTE IN HER DIARY...

"GOODBYE GOD, I'M GOING TO BODIE."

Wild Sage

1856

ONCE A
GENERAL
STORE,
THEN A
DANCE
HALL

GENERL
MERCHANDISE
—
MERCANTILE
—
PROVISIONS

Columbia STATE HISTORIC PARK

A RESTORED GOLDTOWN
WITH TREE-LINED MAIN
STREET THAT MAKES IT SEEM
LIKE A COMFORTABLE
PLACE TO HAVE LIVED...
SOME STILL DO.

44

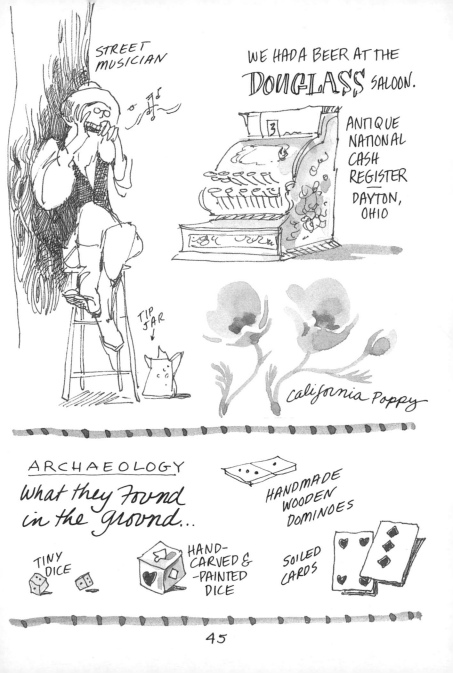

STREET
MUSICIAN

WE HAD A BEER AT THE
DOUGLASS SALOON.

3

ANTIQUE
NATIONAL
CASH
REGISTER
— DAYTON,
OHIO

TIP
JAR

california Poppy

ARCHAEOLOGY
What they Found
in the ground...

HANDMADE
WOODEN
DOMINOES

TINY
DICE

HAND-
CARVED &
-PAINTED
DICE

SOILED
CARDS

THE FRANCO CABIN

WHEN YOU HIT GOLD, YOU MOVE UP TO THIS!

NAME FOR CALIFORNIA HOMES TODAY THAT USE THIS BROWN/BURNT LOOKING WOOD: "MINESHAFT MODERN"

HOW TO PAN FOR GOLD

1. GET SILT IN PAN.

2. MOVE PAN OUT & BACK THROUGH WATER.

3. SAND SIFTS OUT & LEAVES GOLD... RIGHT!

LOVE THE AMERICANA MOTIF

JAMESTOWN

1897

EMPORIUM

A SMALL TOWN WHERE THE LOCAL BAR IS THE ORIGINAL SALOON.

Don't you demonstrate gold panning in Columbia?

yep.

↑ Bells!

PAINTED THIS FROM A MEXICAN RESTAURANT ACROSS THE STREET.

B UILDING HAS NO TENANTS BUT WAS ONCE THE PIONEER DEPARTMENT STORE.

orange butterfly on yellow

47

INDIANS CALLED THIS NARROW VALLEY **AWAHNI**

"Place like a gaping mouth"

CEDAR BARK

GRAPE VINE "TIES"

CONIFER BOUGHS

STUMP IN MIDDLE

ACORN GRANARY

TO STORE BLACK OAK ACORNS, A BIG PART OF INDIAN DIET.

IN THE
INDIAN VILLAGE

WORMWOOD

INDIANS RUBBED IT ON THEMSELVES TO REMOVE HUMAN SCENT—BEFORE HUNTING.

BLACK OAK TREES

GROW 1½ FEET IN DIAMETER EVERY 125 YEARS.

PEREGRINE FALCONS

DDT PESTICIDE MADE THEM ALMOST EXTINCT IN THE U.S.A.

FEW LEFT IN YOSEMITE TODAY.

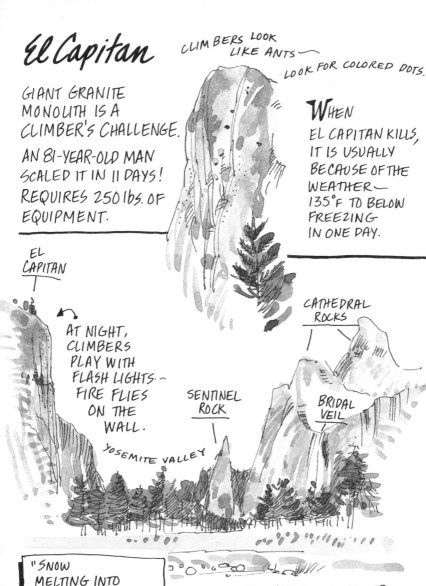

El Capitan

GIANT GRANITE MONOLITH IS A CLIMBER'S CHALLENGE.

AN 81-YEAR-OLD MAN SCALED IT IN 11 DAYS! REQUIRES 250 lbs. OF EQUIPMENT.

CLIMBERS LOOK LIKE ANTS —

LOOK FOR COLORED DOTS.

WHEN EL CAPITAN KILLS, IT IS USUALLY BECAUSE OF THE WEATHER — 135°F TO BELOW FREEZING IN ONE DAY.

EL CAPITAN

AT NIGHT, CLIMBERS PLAY WITH FLASH LIGHTS — FIRE FLIES ON THE WALL.

YOSEMITE VALLEY

SENTINEL ROCK

CATHEDRAL ROCKS

BRIDAL VEIL

"SNOW MELTING INTO MUSIC" John Muir

THE MERCED RIVER RUSHES ALONG AT 35 MPH.

49

WIDE
BASES

BABY
GIANT
SEQUOIA

CONIFER

DISTINCTIVE SHAPES
REMIND ME OF THOSE
MINIATURE VILLAGE
CHRISTMAS TREES.

 OLMSTED

P O I N T

LOOKS LIKE
ANOTHER PLANET WITH
HUGE, SMOOTH "DOME"
ROCKS ALL AROUND.

STELLER'S JAY

THESE BRISTLE CONE PINES
ARE FASCINATING. THEY
STRUGGLE FROM A CRACK
AND DESPERATELY CLUTCH
BOULDERS TO WEATHER
THE WIND.

Tioga
PASS

THIS PASS IS MY FAVORITE.
WHITE GRANITE BOULDER MOUNTAINS MERGE INTO RED,
DESERT-TYPE MOUNTAINS WITH SOME GRAY ONES THROWN IN.

1800'S : STAGECOACH DRIVERS TURNED
THE HORSES AROUND & BACKED
DOWN THE STEEP MTS. INTO
YOSEMITE VALLEY.

EARLY
1900'S : CARS TIED LOGS TO THEIR REAR
FENDERS TO SLOW THE DESCENT.

51

"The Wildest Camp in the West"

AT ONE TIME - 1879 - THERE WERE 10,000 PEOPLE
LIVING HERE. IT WAS A RIP - ROARING MINING TOWN
THAT SURVIVED INTO THE 1940's. ONLY 5% OF THE
BUILDINGS REMAIN. BUT PEEK THROUGH A CRACKED
WINDOW AND IT'S AS THOUGH THEY GOT UP FROM
SUPPER AND LEFT... JUST WALKED AWAY. EERIE!

Things They Left Behind...
UNDER A LOT OF DUST

Treadle Sewing Machine

Slop Jar

I LOOKED FOR TINY BONES.

Bird Cage

Poker Chips

FILL WITH LIQUID CARBIDE

Bonnet and moths (DEAD)

Marbles

CLICK FLINT

Carbide Lamp

Dressmaker's form — and a soft Bowler

I THOUGHT TO BE ABOUT 65 SALOONS, 3 BREWERIES, AND A SLEW OF BORDELLOS.

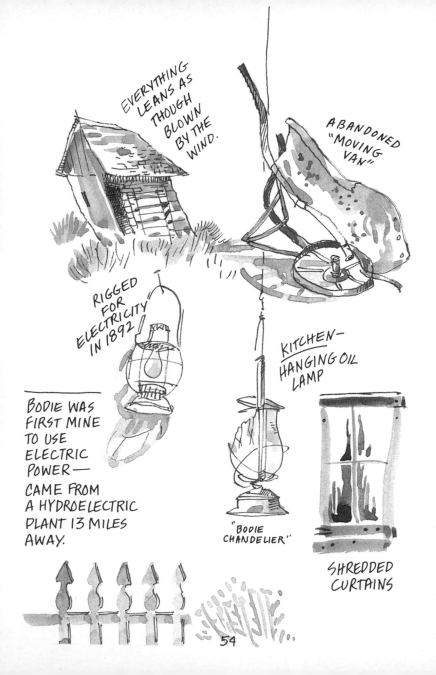

EVERYTHING LEANS AS THOUGH BLOWN BY THE WIND.

ABANDONED "MOVING VAN"

RIGGED FOR ELECTRICITY IN 1892

KITCHEN— HANGING OIL LAMP

BODIE WAS FIRST MINE TO USE ELECTRIC POWER— CAME FROM A HYDROELECTRIC PLANT 13 MILES AWAY.

"BODIE CHANDELIER"

SHREDDED CURTAINS

54

ROSA MAY OALAQUE

very sweet & young looking.

ROSA MAY'S HAT

"SOILED DOVE"

HER RED LIGHT... WROUGHT IRON CURLY CUES

(PROSTITUTE) — ROSA MAY RAN A "GIRLS' DORMITORY" (BORDELLO) IN BODIE. SHE CAME HERE IN THE 1890's (IN HER 30's) & DIED IN BODIE ABOUT 1912. SHE'S BURIED JUST <u>OUTSIDE</u> THE CEMETERY FENCE.

THEY HAVE A LOT OF HER STUFF IN THE TOWN'S MUSEUM (EVEN THE MUSEUM IS DUSTY).

"THE BADMAN OF BODIE" (INFAMOUS MONIKER)

MANY MEN CARRIED A BOWIE KNIFE AS WELL AS A GUN. KILLINGS WERE SO COMMON THAT THE FIRE BELL RANG FOR THE DEAD ALMOST DAILY.

55

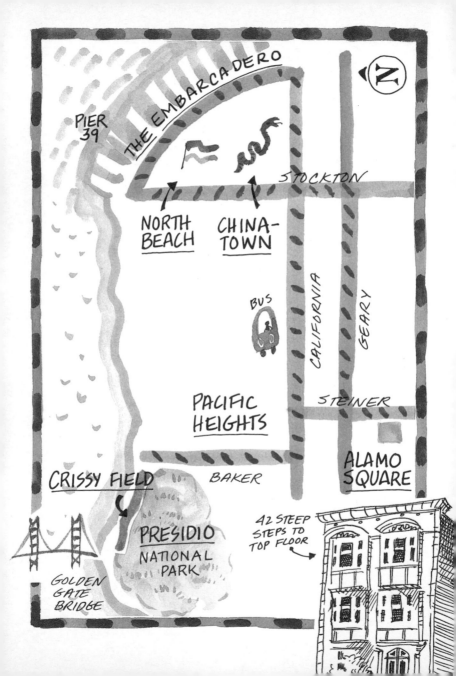

TOURISTS WITH CAMERAS

POWELL & HYDE ST

HANGING OFF CABLE CARS

CHAPTER 5

San Francisco

SAN FRANCISCO'S NEIGHBORHOODS ARE UNIQUE AND
COMPACT, LIKE SMALL THEME TOWNS. BUT CROSSING THE
STREET INTO CHINATOWN AND THEN INTO NORTH BEACH
IS CROSSING FOREIGN BORDERS.

WE DIDN'T EXPECT TO SEE SO MUCH COLOR AND HUMOR IN A
CITY THAT IS SUPPOSED TO BE GRAY AND FOGGY. THE BURNT
ORANGE OF THE GOLDEN GATE BRIDGE IS A COLOR
STATEMENT IN ITSELF. JUST TO SHOW THE CITY DOESN'T
TAKE ITSELF TOO SERIOUSLY: PAINTED ON THE SIDE OF
ONE TALL BUILDING, A HUGE WHITE ARROW OUTLINED IN
BLACK POINTS UP. INSIDE IT IS THE WORD "SKY."

P.S.: IF YOU LIKE TO EAT, THIS IS THE PLACE.

THE EMBARCADERO

RING-BILLED GULL

DELTA LINDSE

A TRACTOR TUG
LOOKING VERY MUCH LIKE A
BIG BUMBLEBEE

STELLER SEA LION

ONE TON

ONE-LEGGED PIGEON

WALKED ALL
ALONG THE WATER-
FRONT FROM
COLORFUL PIER 39
TO WORKING
WHARFS —
NICE CONTRAST.

— EWW. He's got
that foot rot
thing going on.

TOURIST

HUGE CHERRIES AT FRUIT STAND

BRUSCHETTA PASSED OUT ON THE STREET

YOU KNOW YOU'VE REACHED NORTH BEACH WHEN GARLIC REPLACES OXYGEN.

Garlic
Garlic
Garlic

BRUSCHETTA

- RUB SMALL ROUND PIECES OF BREAD WITH GARLIC BUD. BAKE FOR 15 MIN. AT 300°F.

- TOP WITH CHOPPED TOMATO, ONIONS, GREEN PEPPER, PECORINO CHEESE. BAKE AGAIN FOR 2 MIN. AT 300°F.

"The Wok Wiz" COOKING CLASS

SHIRLEY FONG-TORRES

PAUL SPENT A HALF DAY IN SHIRLEY'S CLASS LEARNING TO MAKE

Pot stickers

AMONG OTHER CHINESE DISHES.

WOK WIZ

Shirley's cooking area from an overhead mirror

"Woks last longer than most marriages!"

60

TO GIVE A TANGERINE IS A CHINESE NEW YEAR'S TRADITION.

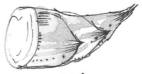

BAMBOO

STEMS ARE LEFT ON TO KEEP FRIENDSHIP INTACT.

Thank you, Shirley

APPLE PEAR

SHARK FIN

WATER CHESTNUT

BEFORE CLASS, SHIRLEY TOOK US SHOPPING HERE IN CHINATOWN.

SHE DARTED IN & OUT OF STUFFED LITTLE MARKETS BUYING ONE ITEM IN EACH PLACE. PAUL WAS LUGGING BAGS OF FOOD, & I WAS SKETCHING THE COLORFUL & CURIOUS...

CHINESE LADY SCRATCHING EACH WATER CHESTNUT BEFORE SHE BUYS IT

61

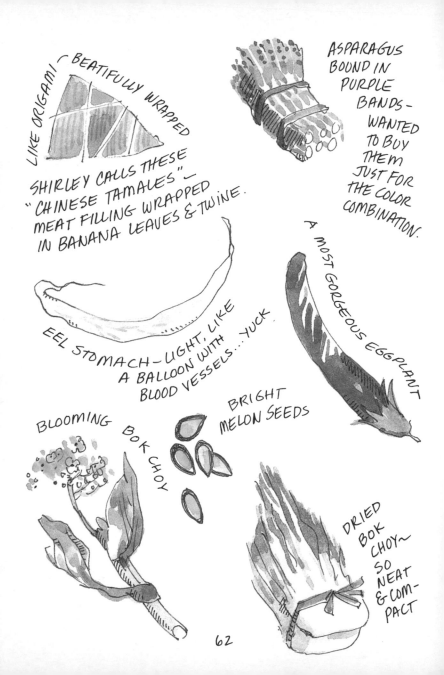

LIKE ORIGAMI — BEATIFULLY WRAPPED

SHIRLEY CALLS THESE "CHINESE TAMALES" — MEAT FILLING WRAPPED IN BANANA LEAVES & TWINE.

ASPARAGUS BOUND IN PURPLE BANDS — WANTED TO BUY THEM JUST FOR THE COLOR COMBINATION.

EEL STOMACH — LIGHT, LIKE A BALLOON WITH BLOOD VESSELS...YUCK.

A MOST GORGEOUS EGGPLANT

BLOOMING BOK CHOY

BRIGHT MELON SEEDS

DRIED BOK CHOY~ SO NEAT & COMPACT

62

Osteria

CUCINA TOSCANA

OWNER WAS FROM LUCCA, ITALY ~ WAITED ON US HIMSELF.

FONDO DI CARCIOFO CON GAMBERETTI

(APPETIZER)

PESTO SAUCE
BABY SHRIMP
ARTICHOKE HEART

PILE THEM ALL ON A BED OF BOSTON LETTUCE.

Noah's Bagels
ON CALIFORNIA STREET

"**OY!** 36 HOURS TO MAKE ONE NOAH'S BAGEL. EAT SLOW."

— BROCHURE

WARM & GARLIC-Y

CREAM CHEESE

the LAUREL inn

LIVE, WHITE ORCHIDS IN TEST TUBES ON THE ELEVATOR. AGAINST THE BLACK BACKGROUND, THEY ARE STUNNING.
WE VOTED THIS "BEST ELEVATOR."

TEST TUBE RACKS JUST 18" FROM TOP

ELEVATOR

WE JUST LOVE THIS PLACE. THEY HAVE REDONE IT IN "RETRO 50'S."

BLACK & GRAYS ACCENTED WITH PRIMARY COLORS.

" *Painted Ladies* "

all in a row

IPPIES IN THE 1960'S BEGAN PAINTING SOME OF THE VICTORIAN HOUSES HERE IN WILD COLORS (UP TO 20 ON ONE HOUSE)... THUS THE GREAT NICKNAME.

OUTSIDE THE CITY, THEY ARE "DAUGHTERS OF PAINTED LADIES."

QUEEN ANNE ROW HOUSES MARCHING DOWN HILL

OLD COAST GUARD STATION

Cute Building.

Reagan gave it to Gorbachev.

Gorbachev?

Calm down ma'am.

ONCE THE COMMANDER'S HOME, MIKHAIL GORBACHEV GAVE IT TO "THE STATE OF THE WORLD FORUM."

CYPRESS GROVE

Pink Sand Verbena
(LEAVES STAND
VERTICALLY SO SUN
DOESN'T HURT THEM.)

American Dune Grass

Grissy Field

TORE UP THE OLD AIRFIELD
TO CREATE THIS PARK
ALONG THE BAY.

INDIGENOUS WILDFLOWERS
WERE PLANTED & MARKED
AND A TIDAL MARSH
THAT RUNS TO THE BAY
WAS RESTORED.

Beach Saltbush

PAUL ON
THE
PROMENADE

Yellow Sand Verbena
(SUCCULENT LEAVES DILUTE
SALT CONTENT.)

67

TO SAN FRANCISCO

PESCADERO

PIGEON POINT

AÑO NUEVO STATE RESERVE

CAPITOLA

17 MILE DRIVE GATE

MONTEREY PENINSULA

CASTRO-VILLE

CARMEL-BY-THE-SEA

17 MILE DRIVE

68

1

CARMEL

BIG SUR

1

LUCIA

SAN SIMEON

HEARST CASTLE

MONARCHS HANGING OUT IN PISMO BEACH — WENT TO THEIR TREES BUT ALL HAD LEFT SAVE ONE STRAGGLER.

CAMBRIA

SAN LUIS OBISPO

PISMO BEACH

N

LOMPOC

TO LOS ANGELES

LOOKING FOR AFTER-BIRTH OF THE NEW-BORN PUP... TO EAT. YUCK.

MOM & HER PUP

CHAPTER 6
Central Coast

WE BASICALLY KEPT TO HIGHWAY 1 GOING SOUTH FROM SAN FRANCISCO, ALONG THE COAST. BUT WERE GLAD WE VENTURED OFF A COUPLE OF MILES TO VISIT PESCADERO AND EXPERIENCE THE 17 MILE DRIVE IN MONTEREY.

HIGHWAY 1 COULD BE TODAY'S ROUTE 66 WITH A VIEW. THERE WERE MANY UNUSUAL SMALL TOWNS ALONG THE WAY, LIKE LOMPOC WITH OVER 40 OUTDOOR MURALS. AN ARTIST TOLD US THAT EVERY YEAR THEY DO A "MURAL IN A DAY," AND THROW A "WE CAN'T BELIEVE WE DID IT" PARTY AT THE END.

FROM ELEPHANT SEALS TO THE HEARST CASTLE, CLAMS TO ARTICHOKES, YOU CAN FIND IT ALL ON HIGHWAY 1.

Ice Plant on the Dunes

PESCADERO

IT'S ONE STREET IS
STAGE ROAD & IT HASN'T
CHANGED MUCH SINCE THE
LAST STAGE PULLED OUT!

WHAT WE CALL A STEP BACK
IN TIME IS "JUST A FARM
TOWN" TO THE LOCALS.

HOEING
BRUSSELS
SPROUTS
IN THE
EARLY
MORNING.

Pigeon Point

LIGHTHOUSE

USED TO BE WHALE POINT, BUT
THEN A CLIPPER SHIP NAMED <u>CARRIER
PIGEON</u> WRECKED OFF HERE & THEY
CHANGED THE NAME.

"KEEPERS" USED TO ATTEND THE
LIGHT ALL NIGHT &
SOUNDED THE FOGHORN
WHEN NECESSARY.

FEROCIOUS
WINDS!

Año Nuevo

STATE RESERVE

ELEPHANT SEAL BREEDING COLONY.

JUST THE MALES HAVE TRUNKS.
BOY, ARE THEY UGLY!

BUT THEY HAVE GENTLE, PLEADING EYES... LIKE

"Help! I'm trapped in 5,000 lbs. of blubber."

THE RESERVE IS LOCATED ON AN 1800'S DAIRY FARM.

IN 1904, A LIGHTHOUSE WAS BUILT JUST OFFSHORE ON AÑO NUEVO ISLAND.

WHEN ITS FOGHORN SOUNDED FOR THE FIRST TIME, THE COWS STAMPEDED DOWN TO THE BEACH TO GREET THE NEW BULL!

GREAT HORNED OWL

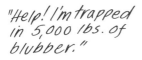

ONE OF 10 RAPTORS AT AÑO NUEVO.

RAPTOR: MEANS BIRD WHO PREYS~AS ON FIELD MICE (FOOD APLENTY, SINCE MICE BREED EVERY 3-4 WEEKS).

Things Elephant Seals Do

LIE AROUND (A LOT).

MAKE SCOOT MARKS IN THE DUNES.

FLIPS AND TO KEEP COOL.

FIND PUDDLES TO SLEEP IN.

NURSE (A LOT) — THEIR WEIGHT GOES FROM 75lbs. AT BIRTH TO 300lbs. IN ONE MONTH.

ALPHA MALE PROTECTS HIS HAREM.

BARKS SOUND LIKE DEEP BURPS.

MATE (A LOT).

She's mine.

But I'm lonely.

FIGHT (A LOT).

OCEAN ↓

↑ CREEK

Capitola Village

CALIFORNIA'S FIRST
SEASIDE RESORT

FUN SHOPS & RESTAURANTS
SIT ON A CREEK ~ BEACH
& OCEAN BEYOND.

AN ARTIST JUST FINISHED THIS
BRANCH & TWINE JUNGLE
GYM FOR HIS SON.

ON THE BEACH

73

STAYED IN THIS
WONDERFULLY
FUNKY MOTEL.

OUR ROOM WAS
ACTUALLY AN
APARTMENT WITH
MISSION-STYLE
FURNITURE.

CAPITOLA VENETIAN

BUILT IN 1920's

OFFICE IS PIE SHAPED & TINY

MOTEL

VACANCY

FUN TO JUST GO IN THE DOOR

THICK, CREAMY STUCCO WALLS IN
EASTER COLORS — LOOKS LIKE
FROSTING ON A BIRTHDAY CAKE.

CASTROVILLE

"THE ARTICHOKE CAPITAL OF THE WORLD"

Steamed Artichoke

Artichoke Quiche

THIS IS THE COMBO PLATE

Marinated Artichokes

French Fried Artichokes

ARTICHOKE
(OR "GOLDEN THISTLE")

HAD LUNCH AT <u>THE GIANT ARTICHOKE</u> ~

ACTUALLY GOT THERE TOO EARLY & HAD TO WAIT... BUT WE WEREN'T LEAVING 'TIL WE GOT OUR ARTICHOKE <u>FIX</u>.

OTHER THINGS ON THE MENU MADE FROM ARTICHOKES...
• SOUP
• BREAD
• PIE

75

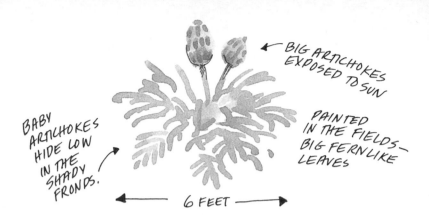

BIG ARTICHOKES
EXPOSED TO SUN

BABY ARTICHOKES HIDE LOW IN THE SHADY FRONDS.

PAINTED IN THE FIELDS— BIG FERNLIKE LEAVES

◄— 6 FEET —►

ARTI-FACTS

- CALIFORNIA GROWS ABOUT 100% OF U.S. ARTICHOKES.

- INTRODUCED TO CALIFORNIA BY ITALIANS IN 1800's.

- 25 CALORIES, LOW SODIUM.

- WHAT WE EAT IS ACTUALLY THE FLOWER BUD.

ARTICHOKE IN FULL BLOOM

SMELLS LIKE LILAC

76

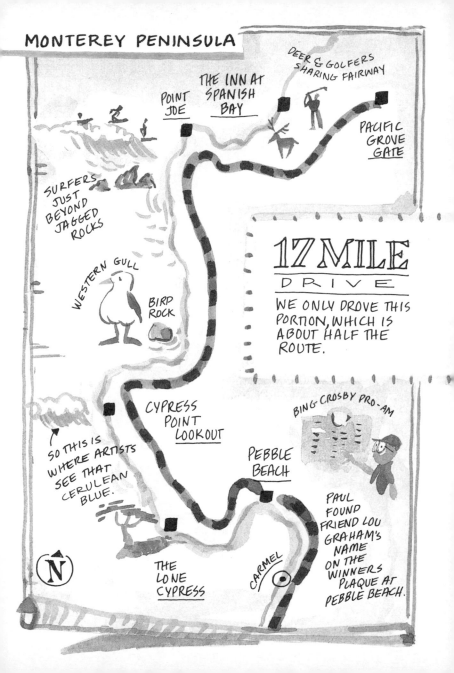

WE FOUND ALEXANDER ZIMIN PAINTING IN THE WINDOW OF THE BOHEMIAN GALLERY. HE'S FROM ST. PETERSBURG, RUSSIA, & THIS WAS HIS FIRST TRIP TO THE U.S.A.

AND HE LANDS IN CARMEL!

SUCH LUCK.

BRUSHES WRAPPED IN NEWSPAPER

THE "WE HAVE WINE" SIGN OUTSIDE THE OUTSTANDINGLY CUTE CASANOVA RESTAURANT.

LUCIA

THIS BLIP ON THE MAP BELONGS TO THE ORIGINAL HOMESTEADING FAMILY.

COTTAGES LOOK PIXIE-LIKE AGAINST THE TREES, SEA, MOUNTAINS.

BANANA TREES~ HOW DO THEY GROW HERE?

Who lives up in these mountains?

~Gardeners. If you get my meaning.

STATE TROOPER

PAUL

GAVE A RIDE TO A GIRL STANDING IN THE RAIN ALONG BIG SUR. SAID SHE LIVED & WORKED IN LUCIA, WHICH HAS ONLY ONE RESTAURANT, A FEW COTTAGES, & A LARGE COFFEE POT FOR LOCALS TRAVELING THE BIG SUR COAST.

WILLIAM RANDOLPH HEARST
CALLED THIS "THE RANCH."

TO OTHERS IT WAS:

Hearst Castle ™

Rules of the Castle

- DON'T EAT OR DRINK IN YOUR ROOM
- COCKTAILS AT 7:30
- HEARST MAKES HIS ENTRANCE AT 8:00
- DINNER 9:00
- BRING A STORY TO ENTERTAIN W.R.H.
- MOVIE AFTER DINNER – MANDATORY

HE WANTED CONDIMENTS RIGHT ON TABLE... NEXT TO THE .... "BLUE WILLOW" STONEWARE

HEARST OWNED FINE CHINA BUT ENTERTAINED WITH THE BLUE WILLOW

... IT'S WHAT HIS MOTHER USED.

This place gives Graceland a run for its money.

TOURIST

CASTLE STUFF

STUNNING BRASS FIXTURES IN KITCHEN

<u>STAGE LIGHTS</u>

USED AS NIGHT LIGHTS ON THE TENNIS COURTS

6 FEET?

A

HUGE CHOIR BOOK IN LATIN

OUTDOOR LIGHTING

SWIMMING POOL MOSAIC FLOOR WITH GOLD LEAF

Loved the green moss on the Pismo Beach Clams

Sergio's
RESTAURANT

SERGIO GENEROUSLY
SHARED HIS RECIPE...

steamers

2 dozen clams scrubbed
1 sweet onion
2 cloves garlic, minced
2 cups white wine
3 tbsp. olive oil
minced oregano and
    parsley

1. Heat skillet. Add oil, onions, garlic. Sauté over medium heat for 10 min.
2. Add wine and let come to a boil.
3. Add clams & fresh herbs.
4. Cover for 20 minutes.

MADONNA INN

WARNING: IF YOU WEAR PINK IN THE ALL PINK DINING ROOM, YOU MAY VANISH.

THIS IS A FAMOUS THEMED MOTEL WITH ORIGINAL '50's FURNISHINGS... AMUSINGLY KITSCHY. WE STAYED IN THE <u>MARGUERITE ROOM</u> (FRENCH FOR DAISY). 15 SHADES OF BLUE & LOTS OF DAISIES.

<u>BATH WALLPAPER</u>
BLUE-TURQUOISE & GOLD SPLOTCHES. METALLIC.

<u>SHOWER DOOR</u>
FUZZY FABRIC DAISIES TRAPPED IN WARPED PLASTIC — (PLEASE LET THIS BE ONE OF A KIND)

<u>SPARKLY CEILING</u>

Daisy Wallpaper with an occasional red poppy

<u>DOORS & MOLDING</u>
IN AQUA.

<u>CURTAINS</u>
CRUSHED VELVET

WIDE MOUTH BASS   KERNVILLE

CHAPTER 7

Central Valley

"FOOD GROWS WHERE WATER FLOWS" READ A SIGN ON
THE SIDE OF A TRUCK. THAT HELPS EXPLAIN THIS JOURNEY,
WHERE WE WENT FROM THE VALLEY'S RICH ORCHARDS AND
VINEYARDS UP TO THE IRRIGATION SOURCE AT KERNVILLE.

FARMERS ALONG THE BLOSSOM TRAIL HAVE LITTLE SIGNS
TELLING THE FRUIT TREES APART. A GOOD IDEA, SINCE THE
BLOSSOMS LOOK ALIKE. ONLY WHEN I TOOK TIME TO PAINT
EACH ONE COULD I SEE THE SUBTLE DIFFERENCES.

THE ROAD TO KERNVILLE IS BOUNDED BY GRANITE WALLS
AND THE KERN RIVER. WITH ALL THAT NATURAL BEAUTY, WE
COULD TELL WE WERE HEADED SOMEPLACE SPECIAL.

ARTISTRY

YOKUT INDIAN

85

FRESNO COUNTY
Blossom Trail

DROVE A PORTION (SANGER TO REEDLY) OF THIS
DESIGNATED TRAIL THROUGH STONE-FRUIT ORCHARDS.

CLOUDS OF HAPPY BEES......

THE ART STAND

A GROUP
OF ARTISTS
RENTED
THIS OLD
FRUIT
STAND TO
SHOW THEIR
WORK — IN
THE FOOD BINS.

86

almonds

Plums

BEE
HIVES
IN THE
ORCHARDS

....IN SPRING

Peaches

nectarines

Apricots

KIDS TOO!

"Quilting is making a comeback."

OUR GUIDE

FAIRLY PAID ARTISANS FROM ALL OVER THE WORLD →

WORLD HANDCRAFTS & MENNONITE QUILT CENTER

QUILTING BEE MEETS EVERY MONDAY. THE RESULT IS A GALLERY UPSTAIRS FULL OF UNUSUAL QUILTS — AUCTIONED OFF IN APRIL TO RAISE MONEY FOR THE POOR WORLDWIDE

WISH WE HAD MET "The Boys," DEDICATED SENIORS WHO CREATE RUGS MADE FROM DONATED JEANS. THEY WERE SPOKEN OF SO AFFECTIONATELY. THEY TAKE THEIR JOBS SERIOUSLY.

Blue Jean Rugs

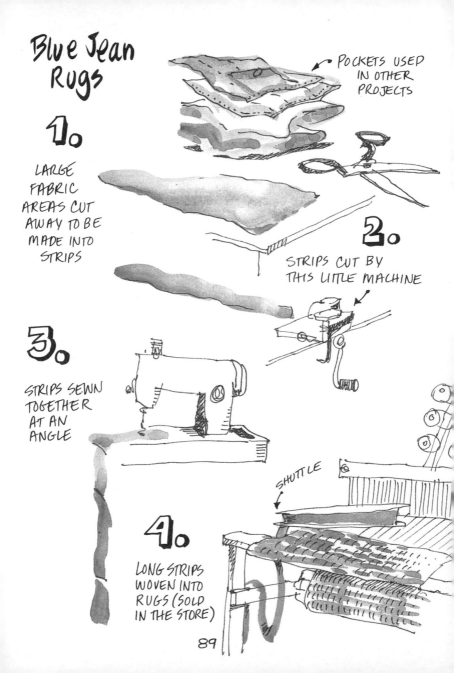

POCKETS USED IN OTHER PROJECTS

1. LARGE FABRIC AREAS CUT AWAY TO BE MADE INTO STRIPS

2. STRIPS CUT BY THIS LITTLE MACHINE

3. STRIPS SEWN TOGETHER AT AN ANGLE

4. LONG STRIPS WOVEN INTO RUGS (SOLD IN THE STORE)

SHUTTLE

The Irwin Street Inn

A CLEVER IDEA. ONE-STORY HOMES WERE BROUGHT HERE & STACKED. NOW LOOKS LIKE A CLUSTER OF VICTORIAN HOMES AROUND A COURTYARD. BUT THE REAL TREASURE WAS THE BATHTUB...

90

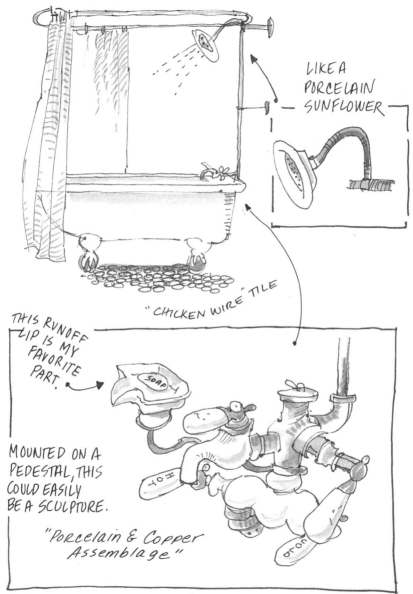

LIKE A PORCELAIN SUNFLOWER

"CHICKEN WIRE" TILE

THIS RUNOFF LIP IS MY FAVORITE PART.

SOAP

MOUNTED ON A PEDESTAL, THIS COULD EASILY BE A SCULPTURE.

"Porcelain & Copper Assemblage"

HOT

COLD

Hanford Carnegie Museum

Yokut Indians - Made baskets from the entire tule plant — roots & all. Yokuts are now called Tule Indians.

TULE = too-lee

How to Boil Water the Yokut Way

I love these small-town museums in what once were Carnegie-sponsored libraries.

Our docent was an early resident.

"This is Amelia Earhart's dress. She left it in my friend's guest closet before her last flight."

DOCENT

1 Put water in basket.

2 Drop hot rock in to make boiling water.

3 Lift rock out with willow ladle.

92

THE KING'S COUNTY JAIL,
1897-1964,
IS NOW A RESTAURANT.

cell locks are like sculpture.

"The Bastille"

3 FORMER INMATES ~ NOW
GHOSTS ~ SHOW UP
OCCASIONALLY.

THADDEUS - HUNG HIMSELF

YOUNG BOY - FOUND DEAD IN CELL

MARY - HUNG HERSELF

I've seen Mary ~ all
white ~ not frightening.

EMPLOYEE

"THE GRANITES"
SOLITARY
CONFINEMENT
CELLS NOW
DINING FOR 2.

Murals give us an instant visual history of this citrus & farm town.

Finding the dozen murals was like a treasure hunt.

To add to the game, some murals had hidden images.

"ORANGE HARVEST"

Mural by Mitchell-Veyna & McCall depicts a local orange grove in the 1930's — families picked while children played.

ALLENSWORTH WAS THE ONLY TOWN TO BE FOUNDED BY AFRICAN-AMERICANS. (1908) NOW IT IS A GHOST TOWN.

Col. Allensworth
STATE HISTORIC PARK

COL. ALLENSWORTH SEARCHED FOR A PLACE FOR PEOPLE TO START A NEW LIFE TOGETHER.

A FEW BUILDINGS HAVE BEEN RESTORED, LIKE LAURA SMITH'S HOME. SHE WAS A SCHOOL TRUSTEE.

BORN A SLAVE IN KENTUCKY 1842

COL. ALLENSWORTH RETIRED AS THE HIGHEST RANK-ING BLACK OFFICER IN THE ARMED FORCES... SERVED IN THE ALL BLACK 24th INFANTRY.

95

Originally known as

Whiskey Flat

...and formerly in another location.

TOWN & SOME BUILDINGS MOVED
UPRIVER IN 1940's SO THE
VALLEY COULD BE DAMMED
& WATER RELEASED TO
THE SAN JOAQUIN VALLEY.

*that
damn
dam.*

RELOCATED
LOCAL

*you planting
your holly-
hocks?*

*Just
Throwing
Bully Bomb.* *

Keith

LOCAL

*MANURE

96

WOODSY PLACE—
RIVER ON ONE
SIDE, TOWN AND
GREEN ON
THE OTHER

Kernville
INN

GALLERY OWNER
IN HIS WHISKEY
FLAT DAYS
CELEBRATION
HAT

KEITH

"THE
SPIT-AND-ARGUE
BENCH"
IN OLD KERNVILLE

"WHAT SOME OF THEM SAID
MAY HAVE BEEN PART CORRAL DUST;
BUT WHAT THEY DID
WAS FER KEEPS!"
— JAMES LONGSTREET WALKER

FROM: "THE ROUGH & RIGHTEOUS OF THE KERN RIVER DIGGINS" *
*GOLD MINING REFERENCE

97

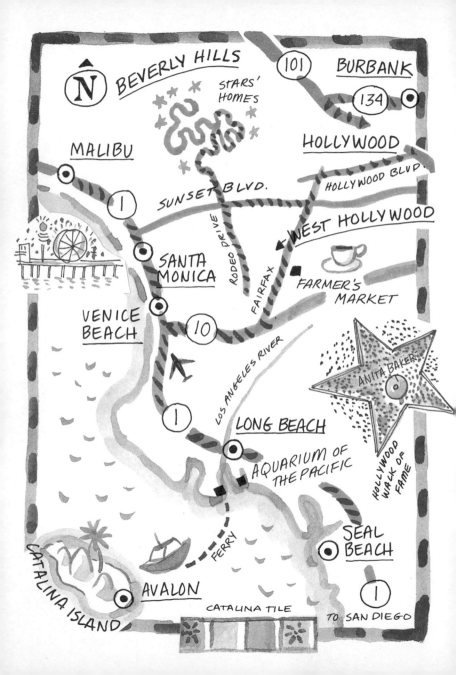

MANN'S CHINESE THEATER

MY SIZE 9

LIZ

(WHEN YOU DRAW YOUR OWN ANKLES, YOU CAN MAKE THEM THIN)

Elizabeth Taylor

CHAPTER 8
Los Angeles & Beyond

A DINOSAUR EYE PAINTED ON THE SIDE OF A 10-STORY BUILDING WATCHED US ENTER HOLLYWOOD. THEN A BILLBOARD ADVISED:"TREES MAKE OXYGEN. REALLY <u>GOOD</u> TREES MAKE OXYGEN AND AVOCADOS."AND A CAFÉ SIGN READ:"NO DRUGS. NO DRUG DEALING ON PREMISES." WE'D ARRIVED IN "LA-LA LAND."

ON THE WARNER BROS. STUDIO TOUR WE SAW CLIPS OF OLD MOVIES. MY FAVORITE WAS BETTE DAVIS IN <u>CABIN IN THE COTTON</u>, SAYING IN A THICK SOUTHERN TWANG,

"I'D LIKE TO KISS YOU
BUT I JUST WASHED MY HAIR."

LONG BEACH BUG

MALIBU

VIEW FROM
MOONSHADOWS
RESTAURANT

SWIM ← SURF →

CARDI

RICK

"FETUS"
(small)

3 PALS FROM BOSTON RENTED
WET SUITS & BOARDS TO
TRY SURFING ~ FREEZING
COLD, THEY SAID.

cell phone →

MOVIE
MOGUL?

B IS FOR:
BEARD, BEACH, BOOK.

SANTA MONICA

AMUSEMENT PARK ON A PIER

SANTA MONICA PIER

LOTS OF THESE AROUND

CLEANING TRAY

FISHERMAN'S STILL LIFE

MAN OF THE MORNING...

... WITH A 20lb HALIBUT.

WILD LIFE

Plunging, breaking wave breaks at the crest and produces foam.

professor lecturing on wave energy... Booooring

101

VENICE BEACH

A STREET PHILOSOPHER SET UP A DOZEN EASELS WITH THOUGHTS TO PONDER.

PHOTO SHOOT

—when do the wierdos come out?

—After noon

sales Lady

DO ALL TEMPORARY POSITIVE EFFECTS HAVE SUSTAINING VALUE?

?!

HOW about him for a Dinner Guest?

CHATTER CHATTER

LIGHTNING-FAST CHESS PLAYER WITH AN EQUALLY FAST MOUTH

I lost a half million in the stock market, and now I'm selling — angels on the sidewalk. It's humbling.

That's some Tumble

Everyone has a story here

ARTIST SELLING WATERCOLORS OF ANGELS

BEVERLY HILLS

Rodeo Drive

"ambassador to Rodeo" WALKING CONCIERGE DOES GREETINGS IN 30 LANGUAGES.

SALES LADY WAS FRIENDLY

(DESPITE ALL-BLACK, SOPHISTICATED LOOK).

← music

VIDEO CAM

TOURIST

Movie Star HOMES

USING ONE OF THOSE TOURIST MAPS, WE DROVE AROUND IN A TANGLE OF STREETS.

(HOW DO STARS FIND THEIR WAY HOME AT NIGHT?)

MAP WASN'T VERY ACCURATE. WE FOLLOWED IT TO BARBRA STREISAND'S HOME TO FIND AN EMPTY LOT & CHAIN-LINK FENCE.

COULDN'T SEE MOST HOMES. BUT THE GATES WERE NICE.

SIDNEY POITIER'S GATE

JACKIE COLLINS'S GATE

BARBRA STREISAND'S GATE

WEST HOLLYWOOD

CBS STUDIO IS NEXT DOOR — SO EVERYONE IS LOOKING FOR MOVIE STARS.

WE ONLY SAW POSSIBLE GAME CONTESTANTS LIKE THE GLOVE LADY.

JUICE

CLAMS

COFFEE

THE Farmers Market

Have you seen my gloves?

seedless watermelon

WHAT A MELON
WHAT A MELON
WHAT A MELON

BEGAN AS SOMEWHERE TO SELL PRODUCE OUT OF YOUR TRUCK IN 1934.

NOW IT'S A GREAT GATHERING PLACE & FOOD EMPORIUM.

FRUIT STALLS ARE STILL HERE. THEY ADD TO THE COLOR & CASUALNESS.

Hollywood Boulevard

TAT-2-U

(TATTOO PARLOR)
ANDY LET ME
DRAW HIM
AT WORK.

DON'T RUB, PICK,
SCRATCH, OR
EAT SCABS.

↑ CARD YOU
GET RE:
CARING FOR
YOUR
TATTOO

OUTFITTERS WIG CO.

WINDOW & SHELVES FULL
OF CRAZY & NORMAL WIGS

Christmas Tree

Elvis Pompadour

Pokémon

Frederick's
of Hollywood

HAS A "MUSEUM" AT THE BACK BUT THE REAL SHOW IS UP FRONT!

OUTRAGEOUS PLATFORMS

MUSEUM ASKED PHYLLIS DILLER FOR A BRA!

"HERE IT IS," SHE SAID, & WROTE ON ON IT.

THIS SIDE UP

MADONNA

"WHO'S THAT GIRL TOUR"

CROSS DRESSER AT THE TEDDY SALES RACK. I LOVED HIS BONNET.

TOOTSIE TRYING ON ZEBRA PLATFORM BOOTS

Western Costume Co.
HOLLYWOOD
Name: Robert Redford
Waist: 31½"

106

WARNER BROS. STUDIOS

LOT IS SO BIG (SOUND STAGES ARE LIKE AIRPLANE HANGERS) THEY EVEN HAVE THEIR OWN ZIP CODE.

A SERIOUS WORKING STUDIO — THEY LOCKED MY CAMERA AWAY, BUT LET ME SKETCH. IN THE MUSEUM, THOUGH, THEY HELD MY INK PEN & GAVE ME A STUBBY GOLF PENCIL.

ON EACH SOUND STAGE:

"WIG WAG" LIGHTS

Stage 16

GLOW RED WHEN SHOOTING INSIDE. BE QUIET!

FRIENDS' SET

IT TAKES 3-5 HOURS TO SHOOT A 20-MIN. SHOW

AUDIENCE MIKE

IF YOU HAVE A HEARTY LAUGH, YOU'LL BE SEATED NEAR A MIKE. THEY CAN CONTROL VOLUME ON EACH MIKE TOO.

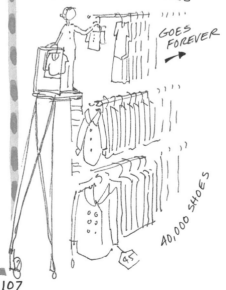

8 MILES OF COSTUMES

GOES FOREVER →

40,000 SHOES

45

Aquarium of the Pacific

Black Skimmer

INTERESTING EXHIBIT, BECAUSE IT COVERS ONLY PACIFIC OCEAN CREATURES.

Black-Necked Stilt

Horned Puffin

THIS SEA LION

LOOKED SO SERENE — GLIDING IN CIRCLES, UPSIDE DOWN WITH HER EYES CLOSED. TURNS OUT, SHE IS BLIND.

108

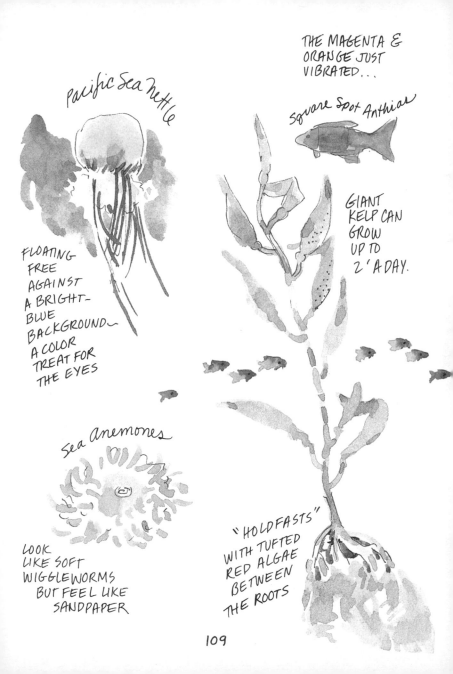

Pacific Sea Nettle

THE MAGENTA & ORANGE JUST VIBRATED...

Square Spot Anthias

GIANT KELP CAN GROW UP TO 2' A DAY.

FLOATING FREE AGAINST A BRIGHT-BLUE BACKGROUND— A COLOR TREAT FOR THE EYES

Sea Anemones

LOOK LIKE SOFT WIGGLEWORMS BUT FEEL LIKE SANDPAPER

"HOLDFASTS" WITH TUFTED RED ALGAE BETWEEN THE ROOTS

Leafy Sea Dragon — from Australia

Pink Rose Starfish

THE MOST UNUSUAL CREATURE I'VE EVER SEEN — AMAZING.

LOOKS MORE LIKE AN ANEMONE THAN A STARFISH — SO FEMININE LOOKING.

Moray Eel

Northern Feather Duster Worm

APTLY NAMED — VERY FEATHERY

Coral Grouper

WE HAD A MUTUAL CURIOSITY THING GOING.

CATALINA ISLAND

GOLF CARTS ARE THE FORM OF TRANSPORTATION— EVEN FOR A VALENTINE'S DAY WEDDING.

CHECK THE LICENSE PLATE

AWACKO

HONK HONK BEEP

COKE CANS

THIS IS A VERY SPECIAL PLACE.

AFTER L.A., IT FEELS LIKE BALI HAI.

←18"→ ANTIQUE TIN CEILING MADE INTO A BEAUTIFUL OXIDIZED FRAME IN THE LOBBY OF THE METROPOLE HOTEL. THE HAND-TINTED PHOTO IS OF THE ORIGINAL HOTEL THAT BURNT DOWN IN 1915.

CATALINA ISLAND
Live-Forever Plant

ONE OF 6 PLANTS THAT ARE EXTINCT EVERY-
WHERE ELSE, YET THEY CONTINUE TO GROW
HERE NATURALLY.

NON WORKING JUKEBOX ~ BUT TITLES WERE FUN.

The tunes
"Avalon"
&
"Catalina"
came from
here.

— "DIANA"
   Paul Anka

— "JAILHOUSE
   ROCK"
   Elvis Presley

— "VENUS"
   Frankie Avalon

— "AVALON"
   Al Jolson

BAR SIGN:

IF YOU ARE GOING TO DRINK LIKE
A FISH ~ SWIM HOME

112

SEAL BEACH

THE QUINTESSENTIAL USED BOOK STORE

SOMETHING SPECIAL

OFF LIMITS
WORK
AREA

Stor-all

B**OOK**
S**TORE**
ON
M**AIN**
S**TREET**
(ACTUAL)
NAME

NATHAN IN HIS <u>OFFICE</u>

"TODAY IS THE FIRST DAY IN HISTORY"
— one of Nathan's Daily Gems

AT A LOCAL RESTAURANT:

WAITRESS

You won't believe this, but there's a kid over there eating with handcuffs on.

PAUL

— Is there a detective with him?

No. His parents.

Only in California!

113

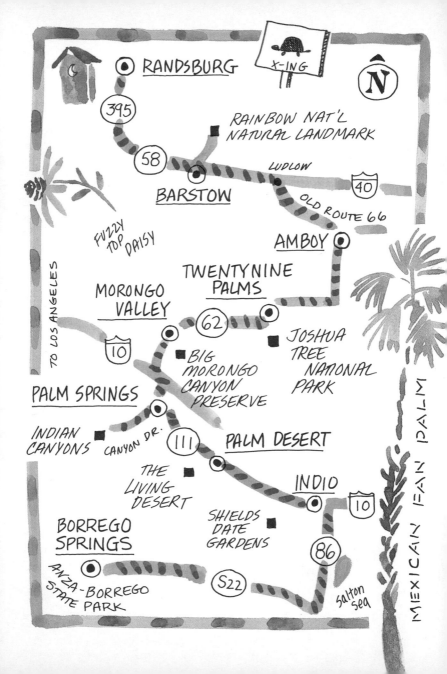

Barrel Cactus

Beavertail Cactus Blossoms

CHAPTER 9

Desert Places

PLACES IN THE DESERT TEND TO BE FAR APART, AND COMING
UPON SOME TOWNS IS LIKE TRAVELING THROUGH TIME.
TAKE RANDSBURG, WHICH IS STUCK IN ITS MUD STREET OF
THE 1890'S BUT STILL KICKING. ON THE OTHER HAND, AMBOY
WAS A POPULAR STOP ALONG ROUTE 66 IN THE 1950'S WITH
MOVIE STARS RAVING ABOUT ROY'S HAMBURGERS. NOW IT'S
ON ITS LAST RUSTY LEG.

FOR NATURAL BEAUTY, WE LIKED BORREGO SPRINGS. IT'S
SAID TO RESEMBLE PALM SPRINGS BEFORE PALM SPRINGS
EXPLODED.

SAW A HORIZONTAL RAINBOW JUST OFF THE DESERT FLOOR.

RANDSBURG

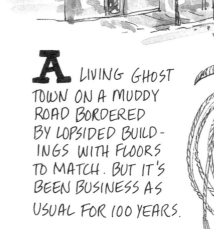

A LIVING GHOST TOWN ON A MUDDY ROAD BORDERED BY LOPSIDED BUILD- INGS WITH FLOORS TO MATCH. BUT IT'S BEEN BUSINESS AS USUAL FOR 100 YEARS.

THE SALOON BAR- TENDER IS A MEMBER OF THE RED ROCK CANYON GANG. THEY DO WEST- ERN GUNFIGHT SHOWS. HE PLAYS VARIOUS PARTS...

WHITE HOUSE SALOON

& FLOOZY HOUSE

1897

BARTENDER

"DAKOTA JACK"

Sometimes I play the bad guy or the sheriff or fall off a roof.

116

Rainbow Basin

NATIONAL NATURAL LANDMARK

← "WINDSOR GREEN" ROCK

RIBBONS OF COLOR RUNNING THROUGH STONE MOUNTAINS — AWESOME

SADLY, WE NEVER GOT BEYOND HERE TO THE "RED PLANET" ROCKS.

THE ROAD WAS WASHED OUT.

House Finch

AMBOY

WE TRAVELED BACK IN TIME TO GET TO THIS OLD ROUTE 66 STOP.

COMMERCIALS ARE FILMED HERE FOR THAT "OUT IN THE MIDDLE OF NOWHERE SEEDINESS" FEELING. BUT 7 PEOPLE CALL IT HOME.

THE ONLY RESTROOM WITHIN 50 MILES IS SURROUNDED BY A TALL CHAIN-LINK FENCE WITH A PADLOCK.

And if you don't buy anything, you can't use the restroom.

PROPRIETOR

(WE BOUGHT LUNCH.)

ROY'S
VACANCY
MOTEL
CAFE

AND GAS STATION

OLD POLICE CAR BY THE GAS STATION— PERMANENTLY AIMED AT THE ROAD

118

Joshua Tree

ACTUALLY A MEMBER OF THE LILY FAMILY — NOT A TREE

TALLEST ONE IN THE PARK IS 4 STORIES TALL & 300 YEARS OLD.

Beavertail

JOSHUA TREE WAS NAMED BY MORMON PIONEERS — THE ARMS LOOKED LIKE JOSHUA BECKONING THEM TO THE PROMISED LAND.

mojave Prickly Pear

ROCK WREN — WATCHING ME DRAW

119

The process, as I understand it.

FABULOUS
ROCK PILES

A HUNDRED MILLION YEARS IN THE MAKING — MOSTLY UNDERGROUND

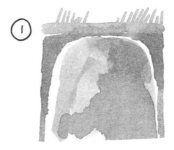

MOLTEN LIQUID OOZED UP, COOLED, & MADE A HUGE MONZOGRANITE ROCK.

EROSION & MOVEMENT CAUSED VERTICAL & HORIZONTAL CRACKS.

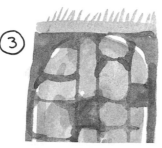

A MILLION YEARS OF RAIN (NOT ARID THEN) SOFTENED EDGES, ERODED ROCK, & LEFT BOULDERS SUSPENDED IN SOIL.

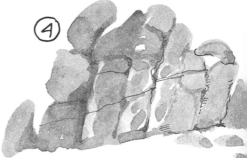

FLASH FLOODS WASHED AWAY THE SOIL, & BOULDERS SETTLED ON TOP OF ONE ANOTHER.

MORONGO VALLEY

THE PRESERVE WAS
ONCE AN INDIAN
VILLAGE, THEN
A RANCH IN
THE 1920's.

6 UNIQUE
WALKING
TRAILS &
LOTS OF
BIRDS
(OVER 270)

western Bluebird

yellow
warbler

Nuttall's woodpecker

LEAFLESS TREE
LOOKED GHOSTLY
AGAINST
THE BLUE
SKY.

BIG Morongo Canyon PRESERVE

Indian Canyons

ON THE AGUA CALIENTE INDIAN RESERVA-
TION, WE HIKED THROUGH ANDREAS
CANYON, A SERENE OASIS WITH
WASHINGTONIA FAN PALMS, SHADED
BOULDERS, & A BABBLING BROOK.

IN SUMMER, THE TRIBE WOULD MOVE
UP FROM THE DESERT TO THIS COOL
HAVEN.

IT'S EASY TO IMAGINE THIS PLACE
ONCE HUMMING WITH ACTIVITY.

CANYON GUIDE

The Living Desert

WILDLIFE & BOTANICAL PARK

AFRICAN FENNEC

FABULOUS PRESERVE. DESERT GARDENS, OPEN ZOO, DESERT TRAILS, VIEW OF THE SAN ANDREAS FAULT, AND ENDANGERED ANIMALS & PLANTS.

GOLDEN EAGLE

ANGIE, THE TINY LITTLE SCREECH OWL IS 15 YEARS OLD.

SEVERAL ANIMALS, LIKE THIS MEERKAT, WERE IN <u>THE LION KING</u>. KIDS WOULD RECOGNIZE THEM & SQUEAL.

Purple Cactus

TIED TO
FRONDS
FOR
SUPPORT

Date
Palm

"A DATE PALM MUST
HAVE ITS FEET
IN THE WATER...
& ITS HEAD IN THE
FIRES OF HEAVEN."
— Natives of the
Old World

ROOT SIZE:
DIAMETER OF A LITTLE FINGER

"The Romance & Sex Life of a Date"

FREE FILM AT SHIELDS DATE GARDENS

48 FEMALES & 1 MALE PER ACRE

NATURE FORGOT TO ARRANGE FOR ADEQUATE POLLINATION — DONE BY HAND WITH A COTTON BALL.

MALE BLOOMS → TO → FEMALE BLOOMS

PAPER COVERS KEEP OUT RAIN & BIRDS.

LEAVE LESSER QUALITY DATES FOR THE BIRDS TO ENJOY.

BOTH MALES & FEMALES HAVE CHILDREN — BUT OF THEIR OWN SEX.

OFFSHOOTS INSURE SAME VARIETY

IF YOU <u>PLANT</u> A DATE <u>SEED</u>, YOU'LL HAVE A NEW KIND OF DATE — JUST AS EACH HUMAN CHILD IS DIFFERENT. SO OFFSHOOTS ARE PLANTED INSTEAD.

126

BORREGO SPRINGS

THIS TOWN IS TRAPPED IN

ANZA-BORREGO
STATE PARK.

MAYBE THAT'S WHY WE LIKE IT SO MUCH — IT CAN'T GET MUCH BIGGER.

SAN YSIDRO MOUNTAINS
ARE MADE UP OF HUGE "PEBBLES", OR ROUNDED OUTCROPS, WITH SAGE TUCKED BETWEEN.

Silver Cholla

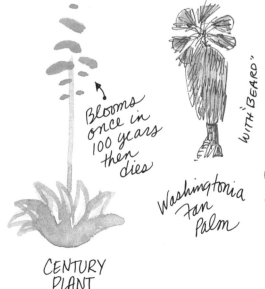

Blooms once in 100 years then dies

WITH "BEARD"

Washingtonia Fan Palm

CARPETS OF SANDY VERBENA — KNOWN FOR THEIR WILDFLOWERS HERE

CENTURY PLANT

CHAPTER 10
San Diego & Beyond

WE BOTH FELL IN LOVE WITH SAN DIEGO. THE CITY JUST
OOZES ENERGY AND DESIGN. THE SMARTEST THING WE DID
WAS TO TAKE THE "OLD TOWN TROLLEY TOUR." THE DRIVERS
ARE ENTERTAINING, AND WE GOT OFF AND ON AT VARIOUS
STOPS WITHOUT WORRYING ABOUT TRAFFIC AND PARKING.

WE WOULD LIKE TO GO BACK TO JULIAN. IT WAS A DAMP
AND FOGGY DAY WHEN WE WERE THERE. SHE WAS NOT AT
HER BEST, BUT WE KNOW SHE MUST BE A REAL BEAUTY.

SAN JUAN CAPISTRANO

LIKE A LANDSCAPED HACIENDA

The Mission

IN 224 YEARS—ONLY 4
BELL RINGERS (JOB IS FOR
LIFE). LARGE BELLS NOW
RUNG FOR EVENTS, MASSES,
AND RETURNING SWALLOWS.

SMALL BELLS ONCE RUNG
FOR DEATH OF A SMALL
CHILD.

PADRES NAMED THE INDIANS <u>JUANEROS</u>
AFTER SAN JUAN OF
CAPISTRANO
(ITALIAN SAINT)

CALIFORNIA'S
FIRST BAPTISM
WAS HELD
HERE.

"[THE INDIANS]
CAME UNARMED,
AND WITH A
GENTLENESS THAT
HAS NO NAME,
THEY BROUGHT
THEIR POOR SEEDS
TO US AS GIFTS."

*SPANISH PADRE
1769*

BOUGAINVILLEA BOUGHS

VIRGIN MARY AT THE GOLDEN ALTER

THE DOVE ON
HER SHOULDER
GAVE HER A
FEELING OF
COMPASSION.
THE OPEN
HALO WAS
LACEY &
FEMININE.

Cliff Swallows

COME BACK TO
CAPISTRANO MID-
MARCH. IT TAKES
THEM 3 WEEKS
TO FLY 7,000 MILES
FROM GOYA,
ARGENTINA.

131

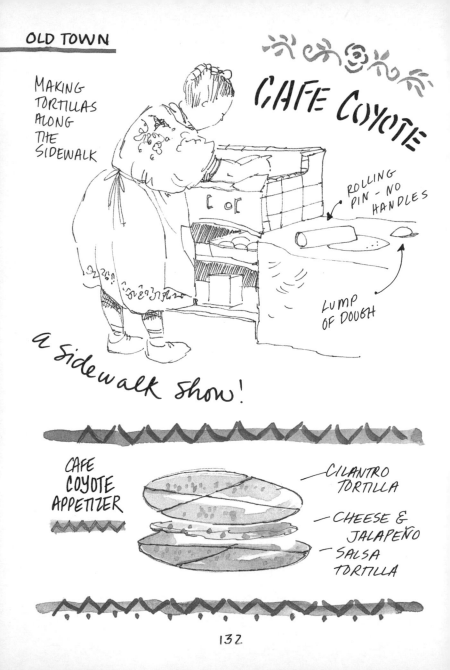

MAKING
TORTILLAS
ALONG
THE
SIDEWALK

CAFE COYOTE

ROLLING
PIN - NO
HANDLES

LUMP
OF DOUGH

a sidewalk show!

CAFE
COYOTE
APPETIZER

CILANTRO
TORTILLA

CHEESE &
JALAPEÑO

SALSA
TORTILLA

Old Town San Diego State Historic Park

AROUND THE OLD PLAZA ARE ORIGINAL BUILDINGS, INCLUDING THE FIRST RESTAURANT, WHICH WAS CALLED...

AN EATING HOUSE

IN 1854 - MATHEW SIMPSON STOPPED AT AN EATING HOUSE & HAD OYSTER SOUP, WHICH WAS WATERY BUT...

"An excellent appetite served for flavor."

KITCHEN SHELVES SUSPENDED FROM RAFTERS

ORIGINAL STENCIL UNCOVERED ON THE KITCHEN WALL

UP TO 18 PEOPLE

3 REST STOPS PER DAY

6 HORSES 5 MPH

Wells Fargo History Museum

BECOMING A WELLS FARGO DRIVER WAS SAID TO BE VERY DIFFICULT. NOT MANY COULD PASS PHINEAS BANNING'S INTERVIEW.

ACTUALLY, WELLS FARGO NEVER HAD BADGES! THESE WERE MADE UP IN THE 1970's.

Six Victorian homes & a synagogue were saved from destruction by moving them here. One is a B&B. Others are businesses. City is the landlord.

Heritage Park

Sherman-Gilbert House. Style is "Stick Work," plus jigsaw & lathe work.

A vase of flowers is where the Torah would usually have rested.

After the Mission chapels, we were struck by the simplicity.

135

CORONADO

"the Del"
HOTEL DEL CORONADO

DRAGON TREE

*B*UILT OVER 100 YEARS AGO OUT OF REDWOOD, USING NO BLUEPRINTS, SO THEY SAY. JUST "SKETCH A LITTLE, BUILD A LITTLE."

IN <u>SOME LIKE IT HOT</u>, MARILYN MONROE WAS FILMED NEAR THE DRAGON TREE.

San Diego Zoo

THEY ARE PROUD OF HUA MEI, BORN BY ARTIFICIAL IN-SEMINATION (GOT PERMISSION FROM THE GOVERNMENT!).

MOM IS BAI YUN, DAD IS SHI SHI.

ABOUT 1000 PANDA BEARS LEFT IN THE WORLD (100 OF THOSE IN CAPTIVITY, MOSTLY IN CHINA)

— Had to draw fast. she was asleep. But the crowds filing by moved quickly — taking me with them.

FEED ON BAMBOO, CARROTS, & YAMS

PARKING LOT TOWER. THEY HELP YOU FIND YOUR CAR.

137

BABY WAS SO CUTE. IT'S ALL IN THE EYES & MOUTH.

KOALAS

FULL OF FAT & WATER

YUCKY FOAM

BACTRIAN CAMEL

THE FRONT & THE BACK ARE SO DIFFERENT, IT LOOKS LIKE TWO DIFFERENT ANIMALS GLUED TOGETHER.

FUR → | ← NO FUR

WHEN PAUL STROKED THE CAMEL'S NOSE, IT BARED ITS TEETH.

— I think it loves you.

1½" TEETH

138

BULB ON END OF MALE'S NOSE FOR MATING CALL

— HONK
— HONK

TIGER

GAVIAL CROCODILE
FROM INDIA

ORANGUTAN

GORILLA

BONOBO

SOMETIMES KNOWN AS A PYGMY CHIMP, BUT THEY ARE REALLY A DIFFERENT SPECIES THAN THE "COMMON" CHIMPANZEE

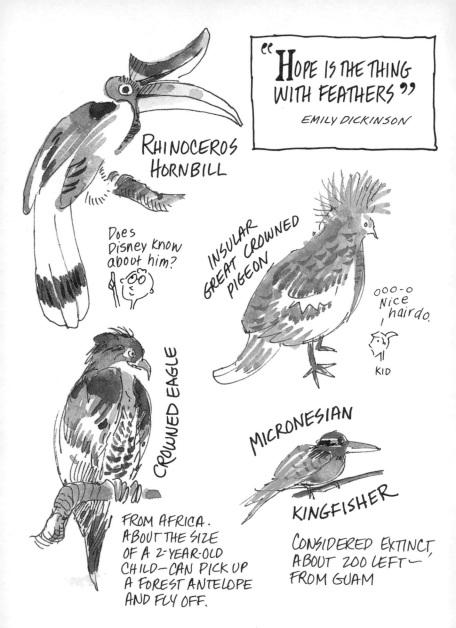

RHINOCEROS
HORNBILL

"HOPE IS THE THING
WITH FEATHERS"

EMILY DICKINSON

Does Disney know about him?

INSULAR GREAT CROWNED PIGEON

OOO-O Nice hairdo.

KID

CROWNED EAGLE

MICRONESIAN

KINGFISHER

FROM AFRICA.
ABOUT THE SIZE
OF A 2-YEAR-OLD
CHILD—CAN PICK UP
A FOREST ANTELOPE
AND FLY OFF.

CONSIDERED EXTINCT,
ABOUT 200 LEFT—
FROM GUAM

140

SAN DIEGO
AEROSPACE
MUSEUM
★★★★★   ★★★★★★

& INTERNATIONAL AEROSPACE HALL OF FAME

THE LOCKHEED A-12 BLACKBIRD

MOUNTED OUTSIDE MUSEUM

06933
933

A SPY PLANE BUILT ABOUT 40 YEARS AGO, STILL ONE OF THE FASTEST PLANES.

93% TITANIUM — WHEN IT LANDS, IT'S TOO HOT TO TOUCH.

SPARKLY!

MOON ROCK
3,750,000,000 YEARS OLD (APPROX.)

MERCURY SPACESUIT
MADE BY B.F. GOODRICH

I COUNTED 11 ZIPPERS IN THE FRONT. COULDN'T SEE THE BACK.

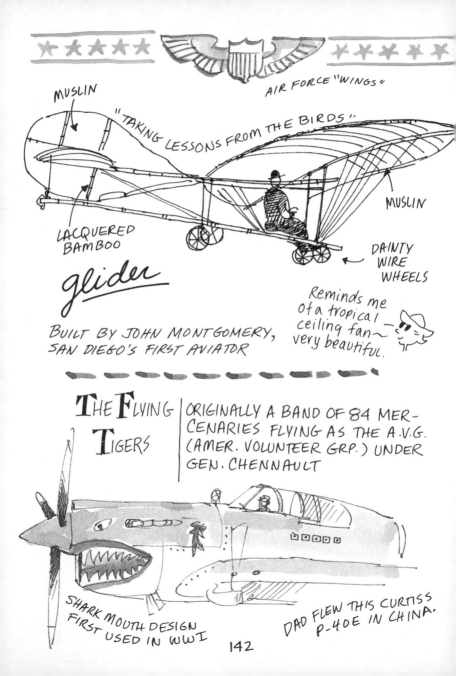

AIR FORCE "WINGS"

MUSLIN

"TAKING LESSONS FROM THE BIRDS"

MUSLIN

LACQUERED BAMBOO

glider

DAINTY WIRE WHEELS

BUILT BY JOHN MONTGOMERY, SAN DIEGO'S FIRST AVIATOR

Reminds me of a tropical ceiling fan ~ very beautiful.

THE FLYING TIGERS

ORIGINALLY A BAND OF 84 MERCENARIES FLYING AS THE A.V.G. (AMER. VOLUNTEER GRP.) UNDER GEN. CHENNAULT

SHARK MOUTH DESIGN FIRST USED IN WWI

DAD FLEW THIS CURTISS P-40E IN CHINA.

JULIAN

DRAWING WHAT I THOUGHT WERE 3 OLD COUNTRY CODGERS ~ SALOON REGULARS ~ THEN ONE GOT UP TO LEAVE...

— Well, better go check my Web site.

Boar's Head Saloon
AND RESTAURANT

THIS IS APPLE COUNTRY SO WE HAD TO TRY A HOMEMADE APPLE PIE.

Fabulous! But they wouldn't give the Recipe.

WORST RAINY DAY
BIG SUR

BEST MEXICAN FOOD
OLD TOWN, SAN DIEGO

BEST SCENIC DRIVE
17 MILE DRIVE

MOST WIERDOS
VENICE BEACH

BEST LUNCH
WINE SPECTATOR
AT GREYSTONE

BEST SHOWER
THE IRWIN STREET INN

BEST DRESSED ROOM
ADAGIO BED & BREAKFAST

End of the Road

Acknowledgments

WYNDY CYTY TRIO IN HOLLYWOOD

Thank You To Susan Goodman, a
friend and author, because she is the godmother of this book
and patiently lit the way. To our agent, Melissa Rosati, because
she holds my hand on the Internet. To editor Antonia Fusco for
her humor and great guidance. To publisher Elisabeth Scharlatt
for saying, "Congratulations, we're doing your book."

We are grateful, also, to those who helped along the way:

NORTH COAST: Karen Pingitore of the Ferndale Chamber of
   Commerce.
SONOMA COUNTY: Jim Pugh, whose son Russ started the
   Vineman Triathlon, gave me all the numbers.
NAPA VALLEY: Betsy and Joan at Adagio Inn for their bed and
   muffins. Jennifer Rose at the C.I.A. for letting me draw in the
   kitchen. Ed Reynolds at the Silverado Museum, who turned
   me on to Fanny Osbourne Stevenson.

SAN FRANCISCO: A special thank you to George & Peggy Haldeman, and Heidi & Don Perez for being our San Francisco connection. Shirley Fong-Torres was unbelievably generous with her time and enthusiasm. Spencer Moore at Noah's Bagels.

CENTRAL COAST: Olga Zellhoefer at Bohemian House Fine Arts. Dan Eller at Hearst Castle. Sergio & Diana Arroyo for an afternoon of fine dining.

CENTRAL VALLEY: J. Richard Neill for a tour of the Bastille. Pamela Stoddard at the Hanford Carnegie Museum. The friendly folks at World Handcrafts Mennonite Quilt Center. Keith Pringle at Pringle's Art Gallery for some local color and a helpful book.

LOS ANGELES & BEYOND: Hazel on Rivo Alto, Long Beach, who helped me find my roots.

DESERT PLACES: Diana Marcum for the Big Morongo Canyon Preserve tip.

SAN DIEGO & BEYOND: Bill Sander of Wells Fargo History Museum added a tidbit.

Much affection to my mother and father who made so many things possible. And sincere thanks to Kathryn and Joe Mondry of Mailboxes, Etc., and Tanya and Rae at Moto Photo for providing such friendly service.

Index

California Seal